Enjoy YOUR BIBLE!

Enjoy YOUR BIBLE!

Practical pointers to make your Bible study a pleasure

WILLIAM MacDONALD
& ARTHUR FARSTAD

GOSPEL FOLIO PRESS
P. O. Box 2041, Grand Rapids MI 49501-2041
Available in the UK from
JOHN RITCHIE LTD., Kilmarnock, Scotland

Enjoy Your Bible
by William MacDonald
Copyright © 1999
William MacDonald
All rights reserved

Published by Gospel Folio Press
P. O. Box 2041
Grand Rapids, MI 49501-2041

ISBN 1-882701-58-5

Cover design by J. B. Nicholson, Jr.

All Scripture quotations from the New King James Version unless
otherwise noted. New King James Version © 1979, 1980, 1982,
Thomas Nelson, Inc., Publishers.

Printed in the United States of America

CONTENTS

COAUTHOR'S FOREWORD

The words *enjoy* and *study* used on the cover of this book may seem like a contradiction in terms to many people. With many subjects—we won't mention any—we tend to agree. But for a Christian, eventually, at least, studying God's Word should become a delight, a pleasure, and a joy. Job and the psalmists surely felt this way:

> *I have not departed from the commandment of His lips; I have treasured the words of His mouth* (Job 23:12).

> *The judgments of the Lord are true and righteous altogether.*
> *More to be desired are they than gold,*
> *Yea, than much fine gold;*
> *Sweeter also than honey and the honeycomb*
> (Ps. 19:9b-10).

> *The law of Your mouth is better to me*
> *Than thousands of coins of gold and silver.*
> *Oh, how I love Your law!*
> *It is my meditation all the day.*
> *How sweet are Your words to my taste,*

Sweeter than honey to my mouth!
Your testimonies I have taken as a heritage forever,
For they are the rejoicing of my heart
(Ps. 119:72, 97, 103, 111).

In *The Believers Bible Commentary,* I, as editor, wrote these words: "Bible study may start out in the 'shredded wheat' stage—'nutritious but dry,' but as you progress it will become chocolate pie."[1]

In that large commentary[2] most of the work—short of moving your eyes across the page and keeping your mind on the text—is already done for you.[3]

This little volume is to help chart your own early excursions on the limitless seas of adventuring into the written Word of God.

Besides the traditional "Bon Voyage," we want to give the same advice here as for the study of the commentary: "Enjoy!"

—Art Farstad

INTRODUCTION

I f you see a book entitled *Bible Study Made Easy,* don't buy it! There is no easy way to study God's Word. It takes discipline and perseverance.

Bible study is all a matter of motivation. Generally in life we find a time to do what we really *want* to do. If we see the value of God's Word, we will really want to study it. But to see its value, we must look through the eyes of faith. Otherwise a football game or a TV show will be more gripping and exciting. Faith enables us to see the *eternal* value of the Scriptures in contrast to the transient, forgettable value of a football score.

Another great help to motivation is to be responsible for a regular Bible study group or Sunday school class. This exerts pressure on a person to buckle down to study in preparation for the class.

There is no "best" method of Bible study. What is best for one believer may not be for another. All I can do is suggest one method. It consists of steps that have proved helpful to me.

1. Pray that the Lord will make you teachable by His Holy Spirit. Acknowledging our own ignorance puts us in the path of the blessing.

2. Then prayerfully select the book of the Bible to be

studied. Probably the Gospel of John is the one most fre-quently chosen. Paul's letter to the Romans would be a close runnerup.

3. Start with a short section. Your eventual goal will be to study the entire Bible, and the thought of such a huge task might prove to be overwhelming. But remember that a big job is made up of many little jobs. You can't study the whole Bible at one time, or even one book, but you can study a few verses. That is where to begin.

F. B. Meyer writes in a similar vein:

> It is my growing conviction that if Christians would not attempt to read so many chapters of the Bible daily, but would study what they do read more carefully, turning to the marginal references, reading the context, comparing Scripture with Scripture, endeavoring to get one or more complete thoughts of the mind of God, there would be a greater richness in their experience; more freshness in their interest in Scripture; more independence of men and means; and more real enjoyment of the Word of the living God. Oh, for a practical realization of what Jesus meant when He said: "The water that I shall give him shall be in him a well of water, springing up into everlasting life."[4]

4. In a notebook write down in question form every-thing in the passage that is not clear. When people ask me how I study the Bible, I invariably say, "With a question mark for a brain." That doesn't mean that I question the inspiration or infallibility of the Word. Not for a second! But I face the problems honestly and ask, "What does that mean?"

Let me give you an illustration. In John 13:31-32, Jesus said:

Now the Son of Man is glorified, and God is glorified in Him. If God is glorified in Him, God will also glorify Him in Himself, and glorify Him immediately.

When you first read this, it might seem like a jumble of holy words. If you skip over it as something beyond you, you will never get the meaning. But if you stop and face the problem, ask what it means, and search for answers, you will eventually come to this understanding of the passage. Jesus was speaking in anticipation of Calvary. He was glorified there by His finished work and God was also greatly honored by it. The "if" is the "if" of argument; it means "since." Since God was glorified by the sacrificial work of the Savior, God will glorify the Lord Jesus in Himself, that is, in His presence. And He will do it immediately. He did this by raising the Savior from the dead and seating Him at His right hand in heaven.

5. Reread the passage often, memorize it if possible, until your mind is thoroughly saturated with the words of Scripture. Often as you meditate on the passage, light will dawn. And you will think of other verses that clarify or supplement the portion.

6. Read it in as many different reputable versions of the Bible as possible. Even paraphrases can be helpful in bringing out the meaning of a verse. Here are a couple of verses from the King James Version, compared with the same verses in J. B. Phillips's paraphrase:

Colossians 1:28-29, KJV:

Whom we preach, warning every man, and teaching every man in all wisdom; that we may present every man perfect in Christ Jesus: whereunto I also labor, striving according to His working, which worketh in me mightily.

Colossians 1:28-29, PHILLIPS'S NEW TESTAMENT IN MODERN ENGLISH:

So naturally, we proclaim Christ! We warn everyone we meet, and we teach everyone we can, all that we know about Him, so that we may bring every man up to his full maturity in Christ. This is what I am working and struggling at, with all the strength that God puts into me.

Colossians 2:8, KJV:

Beware lest any man spoil you through philosophy and vain deceit, after the tradition of men, after the rudiments of the world, and not after Christ.

Colossians 2:8, PHILLIPS'S NEW TESTAMENT IN MODERN ENGLISH:

Be careful that nobody spoils your faith through intellectualism or highsounding nonsense. Such stuff is at best founded on men's idea of the nature of the world and disregards Christ.

7. Read as many good commentaries on Bible books as you can find. Be like a trawler, scooping up help wherever you can get it. However, you should guard against ever letting commentaries take the place of the Bible itself.

And, of course, you must read discerningly, testing all teachings by the Bible itself and holding fast to those that are good. As is often said, you eat the orange and leave the seeds, or eat the chicken and leave the bones.

I know that there are some devoted Christians who insist that we should read only God's Word. They seem to pride themselves on being independent of any outside help, and this apparently is supposed to guarantee the purity of their doctrine. I always have fears and hesitations about people who have this attitude. First of all, it overlooks the fact that God has given teachers to the Church, and because they are gifts from God, they should not be despised. Their ministry may be oral or it may be written, but the benefits are the same.

Also, there is tremendous value in fellowshiping with other students of the Word and in comparing interpretations. This helps to keep you from being onesided or extreme. It often will save you from advancing views that are bizarre, if not downright heretical.

Young believers should seek to have a mentor—a person who combines spirituality with a knowledge of the Scriptures. Bringing questions and problems to such a person is a tremendous help in growing in grace and in knowledge.

Make notes of helpful explanations, illustrations, and exposition. You may think you will remember, but the chances are that you won't.

8. Discuss questions with other Christians and try to get answers. It is wonderful how the Lord provides satisfying answers as a result of diligent study over the years.

9. Keep searching until you can give a simple, concise explanation of the passage to someone else. *You really haven't mastered a passage until you can explain it simply and clearly.* Explanations that are deep and involved often hide a real failure to comprehend what the Word is really saying.

10. Pass on to others what you have learned. This helps to fix it in your own mind, and should help and encourage the recipients.

11. Study with the intention of obeying what you read. Don't evade the plain teaching of the Word. Remember that obedience is the organ of spiritual knowledge.

Never separate doctrine from duty. The Bible is not a book of systematic theology where doctrines are given in isolation. Philippians 2:6-8 is one of the great passages on the Person of Christ, but it is presented in connection with a plea for Christians to think of others, not of self. That is why someone has said that every indicative verb carries an imperative, that is, every statement of fact is linked with something to do. Doctrine by itself can be cold and lifeless. Let others argue about how many angels can fit on the head of a pin; such speculations will never lead to godliness.

*T*HE THREE R'S OF BIBLE STUDY

In ordinary schools, the basics have traditionally been three: the so-called "Three R's": "Readin', 'Ritin', and 'Rithmatic." All others are based, in part at least, on these fundamental things.

In Bible study, too, there are some basics that need always to be kept in view.

READING

Charles Shultz, the talented creator of Snoopy, Charlie Brown, Lucy, and Linus Van Pelt, and the whole "Peanuts" gang, brought out a book of cartoons of young people in a church or young people's meeting setting. It is called *Young Pillars*. One of the cartoons shows a gangly teenage boy on the phone, apparently saying to his girl friend: "I've begun to unravel the mystery of the Old Testament—I've started to read it."

It's surprising how many believers read books about the Bible—commentaries, word studies, dictionaries, geographies, sermons, etc., and spend too little time in the sacred text itself. By all means use these and other sound biblical helps—but remember that's all they are—helps.

15

Some hard-working Christian farmers and other laborers who have little time for extensive book perusal really know their Bibles. Why? Because they read it again and again and again.

A reading program that covers the entire Word of God is recommended, whether it takes a year or three, or however long it takes. Some of this reading, of course, should be strictly devotional—to meet your own spiritual needs. Don't always be studying. Even your non-studious reading, however, will eventually pay off in the Bible knowledge and understanding field. When you read for your quiet time, don't "check your brains at the door," so that you come up with strange doctrines that don't fit in with sound teaching.

WRITING

Always keep a pencil or pen handy when reading the Bible. Even when it's your quiet time, dates of reading, underlinings, and thoughts should be jotted down.

Some people get a wide-margin Bible and (hopefully!) neatly print or write in the margin.

Others prefer to have a Bible study notebook for thoughts, questions, problems, solutions, cross-references, etc. If you don't write down your gems you will forget most of them. Sharing them with someone else during the day will also help fix the ideas in your mind. "Verbalizing" your thoughts—the sound of the words—helps make them easier to remember.

REFLECTING

A third important part of Bible study is reflecting upon what you've read and written down. This is also called meditation. In the original language of the Old Testament the word *meditate* is used for mulling over things in the way a cow chews the cud. One reason false Eastern cults that promote types of non-Christian meditation succeed in Western society is that believers aren't meditating on the Word of God: reading, re-reading, reflecting and going over the words and ideas as they take walks, drive, or sit quietly in their house, yard, or in the great out-of-doors.

In Luke 21:14 our Lord said His witnesses would not need to pre-meditate (*pro-meletao*) what they would say when on trial for the crime of being His followers.

But the apostle Paul wrote Timothy to *meditate* (same word *meletao* without the prefix *pro*). The idea is to take care in order to practice something.

If all (or most!) believers who study the Word of God would regularly practice the "three R's" of Bible study: Reading, Writing, and Reflecting, what a huge difference it would make in our largely biblically illiterate churches!

$\mathcal{M}$ORE BIBLE BASICS

THE LITERAL METHOD

One of the most important rules in Bible study is, "If you can take a passage literally, do so." In other words, if the first sense makes sense, don't look for any other sense. If the Bible says that Christ will reign on the earth for a thousand years, then He *will* reign for a thousand years. The literal interpretation of the Bible is preferable. The alternative is to try to spiritualize or allegorize everything. The trouble with the latter is that no one knows whose spiritualization is the right one!

POSITION AND PRACTICE

Distinguish between position and practice, also called standing and state. *Position* is what we are in Christ. *Practice* is what we should be in our everyday lives. In Colossians 3:1 we were raised with Christ; that is our position. We should seek those things that are above; that is our practice. Our position is perfect. Our practice never will be until we see the Savior's face, but we should be growing ever more Christlike until that time.

OFFICIAL ROLE AND PERSONAL CHARACTER

Distinguish between *official* role and *personal* character. John the Baptist was greater than any of the prophets that had gone before him, that is, greater in his role as the forerunner of the Messiah (Lk. 7:28). But this doesn't necessarily mean that He was greater in character. Mary was blessed among women as the mother of our Lord (Lk. 1:28), but it doesn't mean that she had a better character than all the women of the Old Testament. God the Father was greater in His role as Father than His Son as long as Jesus was on earth (Jn. 14:28). But as to their persons, they were absolutely equal. The Savior emptied Himself of His position when He came to earth to be our Savior (Phil. 2:7), but He did not empty Himself of His person or His attributes. That would be impossible. Governmental powers are ordained by God. This means that they are God's servants officially even if they don't know Him personally.

THE TEXT IN CONTEXT

Study a text within its context. Here are some examples:

May the Lord watch between you and me when we are absent one from another (Gen. 31:49).

This is not a cordial blessing, as often used today, but a call for God to check on two cheats when they would be separated and thus couldn't check up on each other!

From the sole of the foot even to the head, there is no soundness in it, but wounds and bruises and putrefying sores; they have not been closed or bound up, or soothed with ointment (Isa. 1:6).

Commonly used to describe man's total depravity, it rather tells how God has punished Judah until it is black and blue from head to foot, and yet the nation has not repented.

If anyone does not abide in Me, he is cast out as a branch and is withered; and they gather them and throw them into the fire, and they are burned (Jn. 15:6).

The passage has to do with fruit-bearing by *abiding,* not with *salvation.* It does not say that God gathers the withered branches and casts them into the fire. Men do it. This probably illustrates the contempt with which the world treats a Christian who does not abide.

But as it is written: 'Eye has not seen, nor ear heard, nor have entered into the heart of man the things which God has prepared for those who love Him' (1 Cor. 2:9).

While the verse is true of heaven, it describes truths that were unknown in the Old Testament period but that have now been made known by the apostles and prophets of the Church Age. Verse 10 shows that Paul is speaking of something that is true now, not something when we get to heaven: *"God has revealed them to us through His Spirit."*

Otherwise, what will they do who are baptized for the dead, if the dead do not rise at all? Why then are they baptized for the dead? (1 Cor. 15:29).

The context here has to do with persecution and martyrdom. If there is no resurrection of the dead, a believer would be a fool to expose himself or herself to death by being baptized to fill up the ranks of those who had died as martyrs.

Examine yourselves as to whether you are in the faith. Test yourselves. Do you not know yourselves, that Jesus Christ is in you?—unless indeed you are disqualified (2 Cor. 13:5).

This verse does not teach assurance of salvation through introspection, that is, that believers should look within themselves for evidence of their regeneration. Rather Paul, as their spiritual father, is telling the Corinthians that their salvation is an evidence of his apostleship!

Do not be deceived, God is not mocked; for whatever a man sows, that he will also reap (Gal. 6:7).

In the context, Paul is not describing the sins of a sinner but the stinginess of a saint.

Therefore, my beloved, as you have always obeyed, not as in my presence only, but now much more in my absence, work out your own salvation with fear and trembling (Phil. 2:12).

Paul is certainly not teaching salvation by works; rather he is telling the believers to work out the solution of their problem (disunity) by following the example of the Lord Jesus.

Knowing this first, that no prophecy of Scripture is of any private interpretation (2 Pet. 1:20).

The passage has to do with the origin of the Scriptures, not with how we interpret them. The writers did not give their private interpretation of things but spoke as they were moved by the Holy Spirit.

Let Scripture interpret itself. Luke 14:26 is explained in Matthew 10:37. Hatred is a comparative term, meaning to love less.

Stuart Briscoe, a British preacher, shows the importance of studying a text in its context by this amusing story. An old man was walking along the side of the road with his mule and his dog when a pickup truck hit all three of them, knocking them into a ditch. The injured man sued the driver, but the lawyer for the truck owner said that the old man had told the driver at the time of the accident that "he never felt better in his life."

Cross-examining the injured man, the lawyer asked, Did my client come to you after the accident, and did he ask you if you were all right?"

"Yes."

"And did you reply that you never felt better in your life?"

"Well," the old man said, "Me and my mule and my dog were walking along and this man came around the corner too fast, and he knocked us into the ditch. He jumped out of the truck with his shotgun. He went to my dog, and it was bleeding, so he shot it. He went to my mule and its foreleg was broken so he shot it. Finally he asked me, 'Are you all right?' and I replied, 'I've never felt better in my life.'"

BIBLE VOCABULARY

Be sure to have accurate definitions. Don't get your theological definitions from a secular dictionary such as Webster's. Use a reputable Bible dictionary. There you will learn that, contrary to secular usage, a *mystery* is not a "mysterious" or unsolved question (or a detective story!), but a "truth hitherto unknown and humanly unknowable but now made known by the Lord." Any definition must include all uses of the word in the Bible.

In one of his books, Johan Bengel, a devout German Bible scholar from long ago, wrote, "Whoever understands twenty great words of the Bible understands the Bible." We have never been able to find his twenty words so will provide our own twenty.

1. ATONEMENT. When used in connection with sins in the Old Testament, it means a covering but not remission. It also means the provision of ceremonial cleanness when applied to persons and things. It is not a New Testament word, but in modern usage it has acquired the meaning of reconciliation between man and God through the sacrificial work of Christ.

2. ELECTION. God's sovereign choice of believers

before the foundation of the world *"that we should be holy and without blame before Him in love"* (Eph. 1:4). This doctrine must always be balanced by the truth of human responsibility. Man must accept the Lord Jesus by a definite act of his will.

3. FAITH. Belief or trust, usually in the Lord and in His Word. Also used of the object of belief, as in *"the faith...once delivered to the saints"* (Jude 1:3).

4. FOREKNOWLEDGE. The knowledgeable appointment of persons and events before they exist.

5. FORGIVENESS. Remission of sins and release from guilt. God's forgiveness is based on the work of Christ at Calvary. The sinner receives judicial forgiveness by trusting in the Lord Jesus. The believer receives parental forgiveness when he confesses his sins.

6. GLORIFY. To honor, praise, worship. The glory of God is His perfection. The believer will be glorified when he receives his resurrection body.

7. GOSPEL. Evangel or good news, usually the good news of salvation. In a wider sense it may refer to all the great truths of the New Testament.

8. GRACE. God's favor to those who do not deserve it, but who, in fact, deserve the very opposite. It is a free gift, received by faith.

9. JUSTIFY. To reckon or count righteous. Man justifies God when he acknowledges that God is just and right. God justifies man when man repents and believes the gospel. This latter justification is by grace, faith, blood, works, power, and God. *Grace* means we don't deserve it. *Faith* is the means by which we receive it. *Blood* is the

price that was paid by Christ. *Works* are the proof of our justification. The *power*ful resurrection of Christ shows God's acceptance of His work. And *God* is the One who justifies.

10. LAW. Commandment. In the Old Testament, God tested man under law with a penalty attached for failure. Blessing was conditioned on man's obedience. The commands of the New Testament are instructions in righteousness for those who have been saved by grace. Now obedience is motivated by love, not by fear of punishment.

11. PREDESTINATION. God's foreordaining of persons to some position or blessing. Believers are predestined to be conformed to the image of God's Son.

12. PROPITIATION. The act by which mercy is shown because of a satisfactory payment, such as the sacrificial work of Christ.

13. RECONCILIATION. Removal of enmity and creation of peace between two parties. Believers are reconciled to God because the Lord Jesus removed the cause of conflict, that is, sin.

14. REDEEM. To buy back. We were God's people by creation. Through sinning, we became slaves of Satan. Christ bought us back at enormous cost, His own precious blood.

15. REPENTANCE. An about-face, a turning around. It is a change of mind toward self, sin, God, and Christ, which changes the attitude, which changes the actions. It involves not just the mind but the conscience. It is the sinner's acknowledgment of his ungodliness, lostness, help-

lessness, and hopelessness, and his need of grace. It is taking sides with God against one's self.

16. RESURRECTION. The raising of a dead body to life. It always refers to the body, never to the spirit or soul.

17. RIGHTEOUSNESS. The quality of doing what is just and right, the opposite of sin and lawlessness. God is absolutely righteous. He imputes (credits to one's account) His righteousness to the one who believes on Christ. That is positional righteousness. From then on the believer should live righteously. That is practical righteousness.

18. SALVATION. Deliverance, whether from sin, judgment, prison, drowning, etc. It is frequently used of the salvation of the soul, but the precise meaning must be judged by the context.

19. SANCTIFY. To set apart. Christ set Himself apart for the work of the cross. Unsaved people can be sanctified by the Holy Spirit, that is, set apart to a position of external privilege. Believers are positionally set apart to God from the world at the time of their conversion, and should set themselves apart in day-by-day experience. They will be perfectly sanctified when they are in heaven. Inanimate things can also be set apart for the service of the Lord.

20. SIN. Any thought, word, or deed that comes short of God's perfection. Sin is lawlessness, doing wrong, and failing to do what is right.

STEPS IN BIBLE STUDY

STEP 1: OBSERVATION

Some of us have been members of juries. Perhaps more of us have seen jury trials on television. One of the fascinating aspects of any case is the witnesses and what they say. Some are very observant and seem credible in what they say. When they didn't see something, they don't say they did, and when they did they describe it only to the extent that they remember it accurately. Some witnesses are clearly untrustworthy.

Some of us have had our powers of observation tested by training films made by the Federal Bureau of Investigation. We think we will make a very high score when we answer questions about a short film at a scene of an accident. Unless we are most unusual, we will probably get only about a third of the questions right. "What color was the lady's umbrella? Was it dark or light?" We think it must have been dark. Actually she wasn't carrying any! A trained FBI agent can take the same quiz and get all or nearly all of them correct.

When we study God's Word we must learn to harness our imaginations at the point of observation, but not later when we need to use it for creative presentation. We need to train our minds to see what's there and not put in what we think is there or we've been taught is there.

Here are some questions to ask yourself as you observe.

(a) A PRELIMINARY GENERAL QUESTION: WHAT IS THE "CONTEXT"?

As we have already seen, "text out of context makes for pretext!" This is not always so, of course. Many gospel verses give the teaching of the Bible "in a nutshell," as Martin Luther called John 3:16, for example. However, as a rule, we have to differentiate the Bible books we're studying, the speaker or writer, and the audience or addressees of an epistle.

Many religious leaders use John 3:5 to teach that it's necessary to be baptized in water to be saved. The verse reads as follows:

Jesus, answered, 'Most assuredly, I say to you, unless one is born of water and the Spirit, he cannot enter the kingdom of God.'

Yet, in context, Christ couldn't have been talking about Christian baptism because Jesus is talking to a Jewish leader before the Christian church was even founded (at Pentecost)! And while it's true that the Jews had proselyte baptism of *converts to Judaism,* Nicodemus was not a convert but a *born Jew* and also a highly regarded teacher *of Israel.*

Other people use Jesus' words in John 6 to support the notion that we literally eat and drink Christ's blood in the Lord's Supper (but "hidden" under the outward substance of bread and wine). To whom was Jesus saying these things? It was at a synagogue in Capernaum, to Jews, mostly opponents, before there was any ordinance of the Lord's Supper, or any Christian congregation to observe this ordinance. Also, verse 63 makes it clear the words are not to be taken physically, but spiritually: *"The words that I speak to you are spirit, and they are life."*

(b) QUESTIONS TO ASK

The questions we ask are very simple and basic, ones we may have learned in elementary school and perhaps have forgotten.

QUESTION 1. *Who?*
Read your passage. Pick a short one at first, certainly. Who is writing? To whom is it addressed? Who is speaking (if it's a quotation)? Who is acting? Who is being referred to?

QUESTION 2. *What?*
What is going on? What type of writing is this? Poetry? Sermon? History? Doctrine? Prophecy? What is the situation? What is the gist of the argument? What is the tone of the writer? The "what" questions can go on and on.

QUESTION 3. *When?*

Where in time—past, present, or future—is this text placed? Is it in the ages before Israel was founded? Is it during this current Christian era? Is it a prediction of the future? Of heaven?

QUESTION 4. *Where?*

Does it occur in the desert during the wanderings of Israel? In Jerusalem? In Babylon? In the coming kingdom? Place is very important in any historical event. In a court case a defendant is asked, "Where were you on the night of the crime?"

QUESTION 5. *How?*

How did the situation in the passage come about? For love? Because of a war? Rebellion? Careful planning? Divine intervention?

QUESTION 6. *Why?*

When we get to the reason, the interpretive factor is likely to enter in more than it should at the observation stage of Bible study. Sometimes it is quite clear why something happened: It was predicted by God; it was the natural consequence of what went before.

Now let us take Galatians 1 and ask these questions:

Who? It was written by Paul to believers called Galatians.

What? The apostle was upset because these people were listening to a false gospel. His tone is heated.

When? In the early days of the Church. Paul had previously preached the gospel to them.

Where? A peek at a map in the back of the Bible or at a

Bible atlas will show that Galatia was in central Asia Minor. There is no indication in the text where Paul was when he wrote.

How? Reports of the Galatians' fickleness had reached the apostle. He marveled at their instability.

Why? It was to combat error and to defend his authority as an apostle and the gospel that he preached.

STEP 2: INTERPRETATION

If the first step consisted of observing what the passage *says,* the second has to do with what it *means.* Sometimes the text is so clear and simple that you don't have to work on the meaning if you're fair with the text and not out to prove some hobby horse, private emphasis, or even heresy.

Let's start with a verse that nearly everyone in Christendom would agree upon as to its meaning.

In 1 Peter 5:7 the apostle tells us to cast *"all your care on Him, for He cares for you."* The meaning is clear on this one (though the application is something else again!).

We are to put all our cares on God because He cares about us. We may want to check out other translations. The very nice play on the word *care* is from the KJV and NKJV tradition, and goes all the way back to the first published English New Testament (William Tyndale, 1526).

Interestingly enough, if you check the verse in an interlinear, you will see that the two words for *"care"* are totally different in the original. The first *"care"* is a negative word *(merimna)*—distracting care, anxiety. The word *"cares"* is from a Greek verb meaning to have an interest or concern for the person or object you care about *(melo)*. So Peter is making a distinction between anxious care and affectionate care. Millions of older Europeans who were alive at the end of World War II know exactly what *"care"* means from the thoughtful care packages that Americans sent over by the planeloads.

These details *enrich* your interpretation, but the meaning is perfectly clear and beautifully expressed in the KJV by the Reformation-era choice of words of the martyr for God's Word, William Tyndale.

When it comes to harder verses, especially controversial ones, great care (not anxiety, though!) should be taken to get at the right meaning. For example, often people who reject salvation by grace through faith alone will say, when a clear verse teaching this is presented to them, "Oh, that's just your interpretation." They usually mean that some religious establishment—teaching salvation at least partly by works—explains away the many texts that teach salvation by *"grace through faith,"* as does Ephesians 2:8.

Many differences among Christians are *not* that there is an ambiguous passage that various groups interpret differently. Rather, so often it's a matter of how much church *tradition* from ages past a denomination clings to.

For example, in the Reformation era (1560s), Martin Luther felt it was all right to retain things that are not specifically *forbidden* by the Bible, such as vestments, candles, etc. John Calvin, on the other hand, wanted to throw out *nearly* all that was not found in the Bible. The free churches, which never became state churches in any country, were the most radical of all. Wisely, we believe, they did away with such things as infant baptism, established state churches, and so forth. Baptist, Methodist, Bible churches, and those known as Brethren are spiritually descended from the last category.

Let us interpret a difficult and controversial passage to illustrate how hard this phase of Bible study can really be.

Then Peter said to them, 'Repent, and let every one of you be baptized in the name of Jesus Christ for the remission of sins; and you shall receive the gift of the Holy Spirit' (Acts 2:38).

Notice, first, to whom Peter spoke these words. It was to the men of Judea (v. 14), the men of Israel (v. 22). He was not speaking to Gentiles or to Christians but to unconverted Jews.

His first word to them was *"Repent."* Of what should they repent? In a general sense, they should repent of all their sins, but there was one special sin that Peter had in mind: It was the sin of crucifying the Lord of glory. This is made clear in verses 23 and 36:

Him, being delivered by the determined counsel and foreknowledge of God, you have taken by lawless hands, have crucified, and put to death (v. 23).

Therefore let all the house of Israel know assuredly that God has made this Jesus, whom you crucified, both Lord and Christ (v. 36).

After repenting, what else should Peter's listeners do? They should be baptized in the name of Jesus Christ. This means that they should be baptized with *Christian* baptism. In so doing, they would publicly identify themselves with the Lord Jesus Christ, and dissociate themselves from the nation that crucified Him.

This baptism is said to be *"for the remission* [forgiveness] *of sins."* Only Jews were ever told to be baptized for the forgiveness of sins. As we have seen, their sins in this passage refer particularly to their treatment of the Messiah. By going through the waters of baptism, they saved themselves *"from this perverse generation"* (v. 40). They separated themselves from the nation that was guilty of Christ's death (see Mt. 27:25).

Water baptism didn't save their souls, but it saved them from bloodguiltiness in connection with the death of Christ. Their souls were saved by repentance and faith in the Lord. That is the uniform testimony of Scripture. Water baptism took them off Jewish ground and placed them on Christian ground.

There is another valid interpretation of the expression *"for the remission of sins."* It may mean "because of the remission of sins." By repenting (faith is understood), they received the remission of sins. Because of this they were asked to be baptized. Baptism was thus the outward sign of what had taken place inwardly.

"You shall receive the gift of the Holy Spirit." As soon as these Jews repented and believed, they were converted. As soon as they publicly pledged their allegiance to their Messiah in baptism, they received the Holy Spirit.

STEP 3: APPLICATION

The last stage, logically, is applying what you've learned. What the passage says is *observation*. What the passage means is *interpretation*. What the passage means to me (or others) is *application*.

As all too many of us have experienced, many so-called "Bible studies" are really pooling of ignorance. Maybe four or five different translations are read from, and people say what it means "to me"—often with no observation of the context or even observation of the simplest rules of grammar!

But we *should* apply the text. Otherwise studying God's Book could become a mere academic intellectual exercise.

Some of the material is not *directly* applicable to us. When, for example, all the menfolk of Israel were ordered to appear three times a year before the Lord at major Jewish festivals, we cannot hope to do so. But this command, by *application,* can be an encouragement to Christians to be faithful at the meetings of our church.

But when we're told, *"Believe on the Lord Jesus Christ, and you will be saved"* (Acts 16:31), if we haven't done it yet, we should. If we've never been baptized, we should obey that request of the New Testament. And if our Lord tells His people to remember Him in the Lord's Supper (He does, in 1 Cor. 11:24), we should be sure to do so whenever possible.

Some of the commands—such as controlling our tongues—may take years of careful cultivating to obey successfully. But the *application* of James' command in 3:1-12 has to start *somewhere!*

On your own, or at the end of a Bible study lecture class, or sermon, a list of possible *applications* on the blackboard or overhead projector drawn from various types of people represented can produce a remarkable display of the versatility of God's all-sufficient, infallible, and beautifully constructed Book.

SPECIAL CASES

FIGURATIVE LANGUAGE

Perhaps better than saying the Bible should be interpreted *literally,* we should say it should be interpreted *normally.* That allows for obvious figures of speech which we don't take "literally," but whose meaning is real and true nevertheless. When, in the Book of Psalms, the trees are said to clap their hands, we know they have no real hands, yet the sight of poplars, for example, moving their branches together, is a great picture of God's handiwork praising Him.

SIMILE (pronounced SIM-ill-ee). One thing is compared to another, using like or as. *"...His eyes like a flame of fire"* (Rev. 1:14).

METAPHOR. One thing is likened to or represents another without the use of like or as. *"This* [bread] *is My body"* (Mt. 26:26).

METONYMY (pronounced muh-TAHN-uh-me). One noun is used for a related one. The cup is used for the *contents* of the cup in 1 Corinthians 11:26. In Colossians 3:5, 8, 9, our members which are upon the earth, that is, the members of our body, are used for the sins which are committed by these members.

HYPERBOLE (pronounced high-PURR-buh-le). An exaggeration so obvious as not to be misleading. *"Blind guides, who strain out a gnat and swallow a camel"* (Mt. 23:24).

PARABLE. A short narrative, fact or fiction, that has a deeper meaning under the surface. Sometimes every fact in the parable has significance; sometimes only one message is illustrated. Our Lord used parables so that those who sincerely desired to know the truth could understand it, but so that light would be withheld from those who were not serious (Mt. 13:10-17).

ALLEGORY. Similar to a parable but usually longer. Like the parable, it need not be pressed in every detail. Paul uses the domestic history of Abraham as an allegory showing that grace and law cannot be mixed (Gal. 4:21-31). John Bunyan's *Pilgrim's Progress* is a longer allegory, illustrating the journey of a sinner from Satan's kingdom to the Celestial City.

PARALLELISM. *"The heavens declare the glory of God: and the firmament shows His handiwork"* (Ps. 19:1). Two ways of saying the same thing. This is a favorite technique of Hebrew poetry. Someone has said, "Unlike us, they 'rhyme' ideas, not words."

IRONY. Using words to express something other than the literal meaning, often containing humor, satire, or sarcasm. In 2 Corinthians 11:8, Paul says he robbed other churches so he could preach to the Corinthians without charge.

Synecdoche (pronounced sin-EK-do-ke). A part is used for the whole; *"...dust you are"* (Gen. 3:19); or the whole for a part: *"...a decree that all the world should be registered"* (Lk. 2:1).

In Hebrew reckoning a 24-hour day is an *onah,* and any part of it is reckoned as an *onah.* This is one explanation for how Christ was three days and three nights in the heart of the earth—part of Friday, all day Saturday, and part of Sunday (Mt. 12:40).

TYPOLOGY

The word typology has nothing to do with typing or the typefaces found in a printshop, but the words do come from the same Greek word, *typos.* It means a print, figure, pattern, example, or in typology, specifically a "type." In 1 Corinthians 10:11 we see that the things that happened to the Old Testament Israelites were patterns or pre-written pictures of spiritual truths that would be taught in the New Testament.

A type may be a person, such as Melchizedek; a place, such as Canaan; or a thing, such as the parts of the tabernacle. Here are some clear and famous ones:

NOAH'S ARK. The ark's immersion in the waters of judgment pictures Christ's baptism unto death at Calvary. Just as those in the ark were saved, so those in Christ are saved (1 Pet. 3:1822).

MELCHIZEDEK. *"You [Christ] are a priest forever according to the order of Melchizedek"* (Heb. 7:17).

MOSES. Moses said, *"The Lord your God will raise up*

for you a Prophet like me from your midst..." (Deut. 18:15).

THE PASSOVER. *"For indeed Christ, our Passover, was sacrificed for us"* (1 Cor. 5:7).

THE HIGH PRIEST. *"We have such a High Priest* [in the Lord Jesus]*..."* (Heb. 8:1).

THE OFFERINGS. *"Therefore it was necessary that the copies of the things in the heavens should be purified with these, but the heavenly things themselves with better sacrifices than these"* (Heb. 9:23).

THE VEIL OF THE TABERNACLE. *"...through the veil, that is, His flesh"* (Heb. 10:20b).

THE TABERNACLE. *"And the Word became flesh and dwelt* (lit., *tabernacled* or *"pitched His tent")* among *us..."* (Jn. 1:14).

THE MANNA. Jesus said, *"I am the living bread which came down from heaven"* (Jn. 6:51).

THE ROCK. *"For they drank of that spiritual Rock that followed them, and that Rock was Christ"* (1 Cor. 10:4b).

THE SERPENT. *"And as Moses lifted up the serpent in the wilderness, even so must the Son of Man be lifted up"* (Jn. 3:14).

JOSEPH (Jacob's son, not Mary's husband). Although he is never said to be a type of the Lord Jesus, yet according to both Ada Habershon[5] and Arthur Pink, there are over 100 correspondences between the two. This encourages us to look for other symbols and pictures in the Scriptures.

Two extremes are to be avoided. To accept only those

types specifically mentioned in the New Testament is too rigid in light of the words *"all these things."* The other extreme is to go wild with imagination and see types everywhere, even in the New Testament.

However, no type is perfect. Especially in the case of types of our Lord, only the Antitype is perfect.

And we must not build doctrines on types. Oftentimes they will confirm or illustrate doctrines and prophetic interpretations, but they are not a valid source of doctrines.

BIBLE SYMBOLISM

Land or *earth* is often taken to refer to Israel. Thus the treasure hidden in the field could be a symbol of Israel, for whom the Lord sold all that He had to purchase it (Mt. 13:44). The beast from the land (Rev. 13:11) is understood to suggest a powerful end-times ruler from the land of Israel, perhaps the False Prophet.

Sea may symbolize the Gentiles. Thus the pearl of great price taken from the sea (Mt. 13:47) suggests the Gentile bride of Christ, and the beast out of the sea (Rev. 13:1) a Gentile ruler of the Revived Roman empire.

Egypt may be taken as a picture of the world with its attractions, pleasures and idolatry.

Canaan is not heaven but our present position in heavenly places in Christ. There is warfare in Canaan; there will be none in heaven.

Just one caution. These symbolisms are not followed invariably in the Scriptures.

BIBLE NUMBERS

In the Bible numbers have meaning. That meaning can be distinguished by comparing their repeated usage in several contexts.

NUMBER 1. This suggests exclusiveness and supremacy. It's like saying, "It's the number 1 restaurant in New York." The oneness of God is seen in the Hebrew creed called the *Shema* ("Hear"): *"Hear, O Israel: The Lord our God, the Lord is one"* (Deut. 6:4) and in the prediction of the coming kingdom: *"In that day it shall be—'The Lord is one, and His name is one.'"*

NUMBER 2. This suggests confirming a testimony. *"By the mouth of two or three witnesses the matter shall be established"* (Deut. 19:15).

NUMBER 3. This means divine completeness or fullness, as in the three Persons of the Godhead: *"In the name of the Father and of the Son and of the Holy Spirit"* (Mt. 28:19).

NUMBER 4. This is the number of universality. There are four Gospels, four corners (directions) of the earth, four winds (Jer. 49:36 and Rev. 20:8). Four beasts comprise Gentile world dominion (Dan. 7:3).

NUMBER 5. This speaks of human weakness and dependence. The disciples could only provide 5 barley loaves to feed the 5,000 (Jn. 6:9). In Matthew 25:2, there were 5 wise and 5 foolish virgins. It also denotes our responsibility to God.

NUMBER 6. This number is one short of 7, the number

of completeness. Goliath was 6 cubits and a span tall; the Jews in John 2:6 had six waterpots for purification. The best known example is 666, the number of the Beast in Revelation. Six is the number of man; he has sinned and fallen short of the glory (perfection) of God.

NUMBER 7. Seven stands for perfection and completeness. It took 6 days to create the world and the 7th day God rested. Blood was sprinkled before the Lord 7 times in the sin offering (Lev. 4:6, 17). Our Lord gives a complete preview of the kingdom of heaven in 7 parables of Matthew 13 and a preview of our church age in 7 churches in Revelation 2–3.

NUMBER 8. This denotes a new beginning. The world was repopulated after the flood by 8 people. A Jewish boy was circumcised on the 8th day. Christ was transfigured on the 8th day (Lk. 9:28), suggesting the coming kingdom, and He arose on the 8th day. The Lord's Day is the eighth day, a new beginning. In Greek the numerical value of the name Jesus (*Iesous*) adds up to exactly 888, surely no coincidence.

NUMBER 10. This stands for human responsibility. There are 10 commandments and we have 10 fingers and ten toes with which to do and to go. God sent 10 plagues on Egypt (Ex. 7:12) and the master entrusted money to 10 servants in the parable in Luke 19:13.

NUMBER 12. This is the number of government, administration, and clear sovereignty. There were 12 tribes of Israel, 12 apostles of the Lamb, 12 foundations to the New Jerusalem, with its 12 gates attended by 12 angels.

NUMBER 40. Human responsibility (10) multiplied by

universality (4) equals complete testing of humans (40). It rained 40 days and 40 nights in the Great Flood. Moses was tested in three 40-year periods of his life: in Egypt, in the desert, and in the wilderness. The Israelites were tested in the wilderness for 40 years. Both Saul and David had 40-year reigns in which they were tried. Nineveh was given 40 days to repent. Our Lord's temptation in the wilderness lasted 40 days and 40 nights.[6]

BIBLE COLORS

Colors have significance. Purple is associated (as with us) with royalty (Jud. 8:26), scarlet with sin (Isa. 1:18), white with purity and righteousness (Rev. 6:11; cf. 19:8), blue or sapphire with heaven (Ex. 24:10).

BIBLE NAMES

Names have meanings in the Bible. Jacob means *"cheat"* or *"supplanter."* We would call such a person a "con man." He was renamed Israel, which means *"prince with God."*

One feature that has made Charles Dickens's books so memorable for over 150 years is his marvelous choice (often, one suspects, invention) of names for his characters. They seem to fit so well. Who can forget the names Murdstone, Steerforth, Pickwick, Chuzzlewit, Nickleby, and Uriah Heep? Of course, Dickens could make up any name he wished since his characters are fictional.

Bible names are memorable for a different reason.

They, too, fit the character, but they are the actual names of real people. A sovereign God saw to it that major men and women in His Word were given meaningful names—often giving the key to their personality and character.

SOME MAJOR BIBLE NAMES

OLD TESTAMENT

Adam—red, earth
Eve—life-giver
Cain—Acquisition
Abel—Grassy meadow
Abram—High father
Abraham—Father of a multitude
Sarah—Princess
Isaac—He laughs
Jacob—Trickster, supplanter
Judah—Praise
Michael—Who is like God?
Isaiah—Jehovah saves

NEW TESTAMENT

Jesus—The Lord saves
Mary—Bitter (same as Miriam)
Joseph—Increaser
Peter—Stone
Philip—Lover of horses
Stephen—Garland (a crown won in athletic games)
Paul—Little

OTHER DETAILS

METALS. Even metals have associations. Gold is related to glory and deity. Silver speaks of redemption. Brass is a symbol of judgment and iron is strength.

DATES. Don't get too hung up on dates when you study the Bible. For instance, Genesis 1:1 is not dated. The age of man on the earth can be approximated by the genealogies, even if there are minor gaps in them. Generally speaking your profit and enjoyment will not be affected by knowing exact dates.

TIME. There are different ways of telling time in the Bible. The Jews had one method, the Romans another. Often what seems to be a contradiction is only the result of using a different calendar or a different way of identifying the hours of the day.

WEIGHTS, MEASURES, CURRENCY. Here again you should not insist on exact definitions. These things have a way of changing over the years. The context will usually tell you whether the amount is exorbitant, inadequate, or sufficient.

THE DIVINE EDITOR

Here is a helpful rule to remember. When the Holy Spirit quotes an Old Testament passage in the New Testament, He is a law unto Himself. That means that He can take a passage and use it in a completely different context. When Hosea quotes God as saying, *"You are not My people"* (1:9), he is referring to Israel away from

Jehovah. But when Paul quotes the Hosea passage in Romans 9:25-26, he applies it to the Gentiles. No problem! The same Holy Spirit who wrote it in the first place can use it the next time any way He wants.

$\mathcal{P}$OINTERS FOR SPECIFIC BOOKS

THE OLD TESTAMENT

Much of what we have studied together is helpful throughout God's Word. However, because the Bible is a library of 66 books by many human writers inspired by God from different eras of salvation history, there are some good pointers that will help us understand the special circumstances of such varied books as Job, Acts, and Revelation.

You should know that the historical books carry you from creation to about 400 BC. The first five are called the Pentateuch (*five-scrolls*) or Torah (*instruction*).

Most of the historical books follow one another chronologically.

1. THE PENTATEUCH

Genesis takes you from creation to the death of Joseph. Exodus moves along chronologically until you reach 19:1-2 when the people reached Mount Sinai.

The rest of *Exodus,* all of *Leviticus,* and *Numbers* 1:1-10:10 have Sinai as their setting.

The remaining chapters of *Numbers* describe the journeys of Israel to the Promised Land. At the close, they are at the Plains of Moab, east of the Jordan River.

Deuteronomy takes place on the Plains of Moab.

2. THE HISTORICAL BOOKS

Joshua describes the conquest of Canaan and the division of the land among the twelve tribes.

Judges tells of subsequent backslidings of Israel and of deliverances through God-appointed military leaders.

Ruth and the events surrounding her story took place during the time of the Judges.

1 Samuel is the story of Israel's first king (Saul), appointed by Samuel, and increasingly paranoid over David.

2 Samuel. David succeeds Saul and goes from triumphs to tragedy.

In *1 Kings,* Solomon succeeds David, reigns gloriously, then fails. His son, Rehoboam, acts unwisely and thus causes the kingdom to be divided. The rest of *1 Kings* and all of *2 Kings* give the history of the divided kingdom.

1 Chronicles largely parallels 1 and 2 Samuel but as a spiritual interpretation rather than a historical account.

2 Chronicles parallels 1 and 2 Kings, also from a spiritual viewpoint, and closes with the decree of Cyrus permitting the Jews to return from captivity.

Ezra and *Nehemiah* tell of expeditions that returned to Israel as a result of Cyrus's decree. The end of Nehemiah is the close of Old Testament history.

The events in *Esther* transpired between the sixth and seventh chapters of Ezra, involving Jews who chose *not* to return home.

Genesis 1-11 deal with the early history of mankind. From Genesis 12 to the end of the Old Testament, the record is concerned almost exclusively with the nation of Israel. Other nations are mentioned only because of their dealings with Israel.

Remember that many of the persons and things you read about here are types, pointing forward to the New Testament era.

Remember too that the experiences of God's people in the Old Testament were intended to convey spiritual lessons to us (Rom. 15:4; 1 Cor. 10:11).

Rivers in the Middle East today (Tigris and Euphrates, for example) do not necessarily follow the exact same courses as their counterparts did before the flood. That fact makes it impossible to say definitely where the Garden of Eden was.

When you come to the sacrificial system, it is important to know what *atonement* means. The Jews were God's covenant people and were saved—as people in all dispensations—by faith in the Lord. When they believed whatever revelation God gave them, He saved them. But then there was the problem of staying in fellowship with Him, of being in a fit condition to draw near to Him in worship. Their sins were forgiven when they trusted Him, but they became defiled when they disobeyed Him. The sacrifices had to do with defilement. They provided ritual cleansing, but they were totally incapable of washing away a single sin (Heb. 10:4). Atonement (or *"covering"* in the original), therefore, had to do with an outward ceremonial cleansing, but it never gave a clear conscience concerning sin.

Atonement is not a New Testament word.[7] However, in common usage it has acquired the meaning of reconciliation with God through the sacrificial work of Christ on the cross. We speak of Christ's atoning work by which the sin question has been settled.

Many young believers have difficulty when they come to the Divided Kingdom in 1 and 2 Kings (also 2 Chronicles). It is helpful to have some basic information. After Solomon's death, the kingdom was divided into two parts. Ten tribes were ruled by Jeroboam. This was the Northern Kingdom, also known as Israel. Two tribes were ruled by Solomon's son, Rehoboam. This was the Southern Kingdom, also known as Judah.

Israel had 19 kings, all evil, and 9 dynasties or families. It continued until 721 BC when it was taken into captivity by Assyria.

Judah had 20 kings, all of the one dynasty or blood line. This is the line by which the Lord Jesus inherited the right to the throne of David. The good kings of Judah were Asa, Jehoshaphat, Jehoash, Azariah, Jotham, Hezekiah, and Josiah. Judah was taken into captivity by the Babylonians in 586 BC.

Oftentimes, the reign of one king is described in connection with a king of the other kingdom. For example,

In the eighteenth year of King Jeroboam the son of Nebat, Abijam became king over Judah (1 Ki. 15:1).

There were several kings in both kingdoms who had the same name: Ahaziah, Jehoram, Jehoahaz, and Joash. There were two kings by the name of Jeroboam in the Northern Kingdom; the second is usually referred to as Jeroboam II.

Notice that some names have alternates: Jehoram, Joram; Abijam, Abijah; Joash, Jehoash; Azariah, Uzziah; Jehoiachin, Jeconiah, Coniah.

The best way to get a clear view of the divided kingdom is to make your own chart. Begin at 1 Kings with Rehoboam, listing him as the first king of Judah. Then in an opposite column, list Jeroboam as the first king of Israel (1 Ki. 12:20). Work your way through 1 and 2 Kings, listing each king and showing the approximate length of his reign (you won't be able to do it exactly). You will show who was reigning in one kingdom when another was reigning in the opposite. At the end of the Southern Kingdom, allow a gap for the 70-year Babylonian captivity, and final room for the returns from captivity under Ezra and Nehemiah. Save this chart so that when you come to the Prophetical Books, you will be able to show when each of the prophets ministered.

3. THE POETICAL BOOKS

God is the greatest Poet. His Word is full of poetry. This includes, occasionally, quotations in the historical books, much of the Prophets, and even in the New Testament, especially Revelation. But there are five books that are sheer poetry in form and style. These are Job through Song of Songs.

(a) THE BOOK OF JOB

Job is a long poem in dramatic form. Even many unbelievers admire its deep thoughts and lovely style. It is helpful to remember that Job almost surely lived in the time recorded in Genesis 11—the time of Terah, Abram's father.

The principal persons in the book are God, Job, Satan, Eliphaz, Bildad, Zophar, and Elihu.

There are six main acts in the drama. Job's three friends took too many chapters in insisting that Job's condition was a result of sin in his life. They were right in the generalization that sin brings suffering but they were wrong in applying it to Job.

It is important to understand the difference between patience and endurance. Job wasn't exactly patient, but he certainly did endure.

The book does not solve the problem of why the righteous suffer. God reveals Himself as Creator and Sustainer who thoroughly deserves to be trusted, no matter what happens to us in life.

You can find Christ in the book of Job. Try 19:25, for instance:

For I know that my Redeemer lives, and He shall stand at last on the earth.

(b) THE BOOK OF PSALMS

We should see the Psalms first of all as real life chapters in the experience of the writers. But they also mirror the experiences of the nation of Israel. Many of them are prophetic of the Messiah. We call these Psalms Messianic.

No study of the Psalms is complete unless we apply them to ourselves in the changing circumstances of life.

Try to discern where there is dialogue in the Psalms and who are the speakers. Take Psalm 102, for example: Verses 1-11, the Lord Jesus; verses 12-15, God the Father; verses 16-22, possibly the Holy Spirit; verses 23, 24a, the Lord Jesus again; verses 24b-28, God the Father.

Some of the psalms call down God's wrath on the enemy. These are called imprecatory because they invoke a curse. Language suitable for Jews living under law is not necessarily suitable for Christians living under grace. However, when we pray *"Your kingdom come,"* we are, in effect, praying for the destruction of God's enemies, because before Christ's kingdom can come, His foes must be destroyed.

In some versions of the Bible (the original Hebrew and some foreign language versions), the headings are considered part of the psalm and are therefore numbered as verse 1. This means that all the subsequent numbers are one more than ours.

(c) THE BOOK OF PROVERBS

First, it is good to know what a proverb is. It is a short

saying of truth or wisdom that is stated in such a way as to be easy to remember.

The chief purpose of Proverbs is to teach wisdom.

There seems to be a flow of thought in the first nine chapters (two women are prominent), in 16:1-11 (guidance), in chapter 24 (note the repetition of "do not"), and in the last two. Most of the rest of the book seems to be made up of isolated proverbs without any obvious connection. However, there may be order that we do not discern. Always allow for that possibility in studying any part of the Bible.

Through the centuries, many believers have read a chapter a day in Proverbs. The book has one chapter for every day in the month, and continual reading and re-reading will increase one's grasp of wisdom and discernment for daily living.

(d) THE BOOK OF ECCLESIASTES

This is a beautiful but puzzling book until you put the key in the door. The key is the phrase *"under the sun,"* occurring 29 times.

This is Solomon's search under the sun for the meaning of life. He tries to find fulfillment in education, materialism, pleasure, wine, sex, entertainment, and everything else possible, but comes to the dismal conclusion that nothing in the world can satisfy the human heart. All is vanity and a chasing after wind.

The name for God found in this book is *Elohim,* but never the name *Jehovah* (the covenant-keeping God). A man can know there is an Elohim (Mighty One) by the works of creation, but he can only know Jehovah by divine revelation.

Because it is man's thinking apart from divine revelation, some conclusions in it are true, some are only half true, and some are not true at all. However, this does not affect the fact that the book is inspired. Inspiration does not guarantee the accuracy of what Satan says or what man says *"under the sun."*

(e) THE SONG OF SOLOMON

Because the song is found in the Old Testament, its interpretation must deal with Israel, not with the Church. Perhaps spiritual applications may be made to Christ's love for the Church, but that is not the primary message.

The key verse is found three times:

I charge you, O daughters of Jerusalem...do not stir up nor awaken love until it pleases (2:7; 3:5; 8:4).

The song is a protest against unfaithfulness in the marriage relationship. Israel was married to the Lord but had been unfaithful to Him and had run after idols.

The original language of the Old Testament usually indicates whether the person addressed is male or female, and whether one person is spoken to or more. Some modern Bible versions indicate the sex and number.

The principal characters are the Shulamite, the daughters of Jerusalem, Solomon, and an unnamed shepherd.[8]

When Solomon is in view, everything speaks of luxury, magnificence, and royalty. When the shepherd lover comes on stage, the setting is rural and pastoral.

Solomon seeks to woo and win the Shulamite as an addition to his harem. But she is consistently impervious to his charms. Then in the last chapter, her lover appears to claim her as his own.

4. THE PROPHETS

The prophets were spokesmen or mouthpieces of God. The Lord raised them up in times of sin and declension to cry out against the prevailing evils, to call the people back, to warn about the consequences of rebellion (especially the captivity), and to promise blessing through obedience (especially the return from captivity). Therefore, they were first *forth*tellers, then *fore*tellers.

The Old Testament prophets are generally classified:

MAJOR: Isaiah, Jeremiah (including his Lamentations), Ezekiel, and Daniel.
MINOR: All the rest.

We should note that the words *major* and *minor,* as applied to the prophets, do *not* mean important and unimportant! For example, Zechariah, a "Minor Prophet," is very important in its messianic predictions. The words refer only to size. Technically, Daniel was not a "prophet" by calling, but a government official who was gifted by God in prophecy. In the Hebrew Bible, Daniel is in their third section, called "The Writings."

They can also be classified according to the time they prophesied.

i) BEFORE the BABYLONIAN CAPTIVITY, also called PRE-

EXILIC: Isaiah, Jeremiah, Hosea, Joel, Amos, Obadiah, Jonah, Micah, Nahum, Habakkuk, Zephaniah.

ii) DURING the BABYLONIAN CAPTIVITY, i.e., EXILIC: Ezekiel, Daniel.

iii) AFTER the BABYLONIAN CAPTIVITY, or POST-EXILIC: Haggai, Zechariah, Malachi.

An easy way to remember which category any prophet belongs to is this: The last three prophets of the Old Testament were last, writing *after* the exile (Post-exilic). Ezekiel and Daniel wrote *during* the exile (Exilic). All the rest wrote *before* the exile (Pre-exilic).

Some ministered to Israel, some to Judah, one—Jonah—to a Gentile nation, and some to a combination of these. The lines here are not so clear, and the classification not so exact.

If you made a chart of the Divided Kingdom, as suggested previously, this would be a good time to fill in the prophets at the time when each one ministered.

(a) NAMES PROMINENT IN THE PROPHETS

You will become familiar with the following names:
JERUSALEM—sometimes called Zion, the capital of Judah.

SAMARIA—the capital of Israel.

ISRAEL—sometimes used of the ten northern tribes, sometimes of the entire nation. Ephraim is also used in Hosea as another name for the northern kingdom.

ASSYRIA—a bitter and cruel enemy of Israel. The King of the North ruled here.

NINEVEH—capital of Assyria.

SYRIA—another enemy nation.

DAMASCUS—a city-state associated with Syria.

EGYPT—ruled by the King of the South.

BABYLONIA, BABYLON, CHALDEA—names sometimes used interchangeably. Babylon was the city.

(b) TRANSITIONS IN TIME

In studying the prophets—who were also quite poetic—you must get used to quick transitions. One moment they will be thundering out the coming judgments of the Lord (Joel 3:14-16), then abruptly they will switch to the glories of the coming kingdom (Joel 3:17-18). In the same passage they can move from the Messiah's first advent (Isa. 52:14) to His second (Isa. 52:15) with nothing more than a semicolon separating them!

(c) THE DAY OF THE LORD

The *"day of the Lord"* is not a 24-hour period but covers centuries. In the Old Testament, it referred to any time when God defeated Israel's enemies or punished His own people. In the New Testament, the day of the Lord begins after the Rapture and includes the Tribulation, the Second Coming, the Millennium, and the final destruction of the heaven and earth with fire.

(d) LAW OF DOUBLE REFERENCE

You will want to be on the lookout for the law of double reference. This means that a prophecy may have an early and partial fulfillment, then a later and complete fulfillment. The classic example is Joel's prophecy in 2:28-32. This was partially fulfilled at Pentecost when the Spirit was poured out on a company of Jewish believers in their Messiah, but it will be completely fulfilled at Christ's Second Advent when He will pour out the Holy Spirit on all flesh.

(e) FALSE PROPHETS

In addition to the prophets of God, there were also false prophets. They always prophesied peace and prosperity in times of sin and rebellion. Times haven't changed!

THE NEW TESTAMENT

1. THE GOSPELS

The Gospels are perhaps the most familiar part of the Bible. Yet few Christians really understand their scope and purpose.

These books do not attempt to give a full account of the life of Christ; that would be impossible (Jn. 21:25). With the exception of five chapters, they are devoted to the last three years of His life (84 out of 89). Twenty-eight chapters are devoted to the 10 days between His final arrival in Bethany and His resurrection (28 out of 89).

Some incidents are found in one, two, or three Gospels. The feeding of the 5,000 is in all four.

Incidents are not always related in the same order. Some are:

CHRONOLOGICAL—arranged by the time sequence in which they occurred.

DISPENSATIONAL—Matthew 8:1-17. Notice four miracles. The first, where Jesus is bodily present, pictures Him on earth, ministering to the sick house of Israel. In the second, Jesus is not present but He heals a Gentile. When He heals Peter's Jewish mother-in-law, He is present. Finally He heals the multitude. These four miracles may well picture the Lord's earthly ministry, then His healing work during this age of grace. This will be followed by the restoration of Israel at His Second Coming. And finally you have His ministry during the Millennium.

MORAL OR SPIRITUAL—Matthew 9:23-24. The dead is raised. Blind eyes are given sight. Dumb lips are opened in testimony. Is this not the order when a person is saved?

In John's Gospel, events lead up to a discourse or saying of the Lord. For example, in John 12:20-26, the visit of the Greeks led to the Savior's words about a grain of wheat.

Each of the Gospels is designed to present the Lord Jesus in a different aspect:

Gospel	Jesus as:	Symbol[9]	Color
MATTHEW	King	Lion	Purple (Jud. 8:26)
MARK	Servant	Ox, calf	Scarlet (Ps. 22:6)[10]
LUKE	Man	Man	White (Rev. 19:8)
JOHN	God	Eagle	Blue/sapphire (Ex. 24:10)

There are two other ways in which the four Gospels are depicted:

Gospel	The Branch (or son)	Behold!
MATTHEW	The Branch of David (Jer. 23:5-6)	Behold, your King (Zech. 9:9)
MARK	My servant, the Branch (Zech. 3:8)	Behold! My Servant (Isa. 42:1; 52:13)
LUKE	The man...the Branch (Zech. 6:12)	Behold, the Man (Zech. 6:12)
JOHN	The Branch of Jehovah (Isa. 4:2)	Behold, your God (Isa. 40:9)

There is no way that human writers could have collaborated to produce these fourfold presentations of the Lord Jesus as He would be portrayed centuries later in the four Gospels.

The Holy Spirit selects material on this basis. For instance, there is no genealogy in Mark or John. Such would be unnecessary for a slave and nonexistent for the eternal Son of God. But it is important for Jesus as King (Matthew) and as Son of Man (Luke).

Sometimes what seems to be the same incident recorded in different Gospels is actually different. The cleansing of the temple in John 2:13-25 took place at the beginning of Jesus' public ministry, the one in Matthew, Mark and Luke at the close.

Differences in Gospel accounts of the same event are not contradictory. Sometimes they are supplementary. To get the complete superscription on the Savior's Cross, combine the ones that are given in the four Gospels and you will get, *"This is Jesus of Nazareth, the King of the Jews."*

The reason for differences is always significant and meaningful. For instance, in Matthew 10:24, Jesus is the Teacher and Master and we are the disciples and servants. In the companion passage, Luke 6:40, we are the teacher and the one we are trying to teach is the disciple. Again in Matthew 7:22, unbelievers are professing service to the King, whereas in Luke 13:26, they are professing fellowship with the Man. The story of the 99 in Matthew 18:12-13 emphasizes the Lord's care for His little ones, while in Luke 15:11-7, it condemns the Pharisees who sensed no need of repentance.

It seems to us that people largely miss the point when they write books seeking to *harmonize* the Gospels. It's not the similarities that are significant but the *differences.* The Holy Spirit never needlessly repeats Himself.

Jesus' public ministry can be divided into three phases:

HIS JUDEAN MINISTRY, about 1 year (Jn. 1:154:54).

HIS GALILEAN MINISTRY, about 1 year, 9 months (Mt. 4:12–18:35; Mk. 1:14–9:50; Lk. 3:19–9:50; Jn. 5:1–10:21).

HIS PEREAN MINISTRY, four or five months (Jn. 10:22–11:57).

The first three Gospels are called synoptics ("seen together" in Greek), because generally speaking they cover the same ground.

John's Gospel is called *autoptic.* Over 90% of the material he uses is unique to his Gospel.

Except for John, the Gospels are not so much a presentation of the way of salvation as they are a historical record of the events by which salvation was made possible. Of course, in all of them there are individual verses that teach salvation by faith in Christ, but you have to wait until you get to Romans to find the doctrine of salvation expounded.

(a) UNDERSTANDING THE OLIVET DISCOURSE

Suppose you were reading Matthew 24 and 25 for the first time. You would be electrified by the dramatic events described in it. But you would be mystified as well. All kinds of questions would arise in your mind. Who? When? How does all this apply to me?

There are four main keys to unlocking the discourse.

1. The discourse has to do with Israel, not the Church. In fact, the Church is not referred to once in the Olivet Discourse. Note the Jewish references: the holy place, that is, the temple in Jerusalem (24:15); Judea (24:16). and not travelling a great distance on the Sabbath (24:20).

Don't be thrown off by references to *"the elect"* (24:22, 24, 31). These refer to God's Jewish elect (chosen ones) during the Tribulation. The elect of the church period will already have been raptured home to heaven.

Likewise "the brethren" in 25:40 are the Lord's *Jewish* brethren.

2. The discourse has to do with the prophetic future,

not with history or coming events.

   a. The Tribulation (24:4-28).

   b. The Second Advent (24:30).

   c. The Judgment of the Nations (25:31-46).

   3. The gospel mentioned in the Olivet Discourse (24:14) is the gospel of the kingdom, not the gospel of the grace of God.

This does not contradict the fact that there is only one gospel—salvation by faith in the Lord. But there are different emphases and different administrations of the gospel in different ages. In the Old Testament era people were saved by believing whatever revelation God gave to them. Today we are saved by faith in Christ with the promise that He will take us to heaven when He returns. The emphasis in the Tribulation will be, "Believe on the Lord Jesus Christ and you will be saved, and when He returns, you will enter the kingdom with Him." That is the gospel, or good news, about the kingdom.

   4. The discourse has to do with Christ's coming to reign, not with the Rapture. It will be preceded by celestial disturbances, will be accompanied by fearful judgments, and resurrection is not emphasized. There are no signs in the heavens before the Rapture. There are no judgments at the Rapture. And resurrection is one of the prominent features of the Rapture.

In 24:40-41, those who are taken away are taken in judgment. Those who are left are the ones who enter the kingdom. This is just the opposite to what happens at the Rapture of the Church. In 25:13, the foolish virgins are professing Jews in the Tribulation who never were truly born again. The wise virgins are believing Jews who go in to the wedding feast at the time of the Second Advent.

Although the interpretation of the Olivet Discourse has to do with Israel and the nations, that does not mean it has no message for us today. It tells us we are in the last days, that the Lord's coming draws near, that we should be watching and waiting, and that we should be actively evangelizing so that people will be saved from the coming wrath.

(b) RED-LETTER BIBLES

One final word! Bibles that print the words of Jesus in red letters also miss the point. They seem to imply that His words are more important, more inspired than others. The fact is that there are no degrees of inspiration. The Bible is inspired from cover to cover. (If, however, you are making a study of all the words of our Lord, the red-letter makes it much easier to find them.)

2. THE BOOK OF ACTS

J. B. Phillips called this book, *The Young Church in Action.* That's a good title; we wish we had thought of it. The book has also been called, *The Acts of the Holy Spirit.* That too describes it well.

The narrative covers about 34 years—from the ascension of Christ to Paul's first imprisonment, AD 30-63.

Peter occupies the key role in chapters 1-12. After that, Paul takes center stage. The text does not profess to give a complete history, but only isolated events chosen by the

Holy Spirit to trace the spiritual development of the early Church.

Some of the more important sections are as follows:

AD 30-37	From the ascension of Christ to the martyrdom of Stephen (chs. 1–8).
AD 37-40	From the conversion of Saul to his first visit to Jerusalem (ch. 9).
AD 40-42	From the conversion of Cornelius to Paul's arrival at Antioch (chs. 10–11).
AD 44	From the martyrdom of James to the death of Herod (Ch. 12).
AD 45-47	Paul's first missionary journey (chs. 13-14).
AD 48	Interim between missionary journeys, including the council at Jerusalem (ch. 15).
AD 50-54	Paul's second missionary journey (chs. 16–18).
AD 54-58	Paul's third missionary journey (chs. 19-21).
AD 58-60	Paul's imprisonment at Caesarea (chs. 22–26).
AD 60-63	Paul's voyage to Rome and imprisonment there (chs. 27–28).

Acts describes the historic fulfillment of Christ's command that the gospel should be preached to the Jew first, then to the Gentile (1:8). The audiences in the early chapters are Jewish, but as the majority of God's ancient people consistently reject the message, the gospel goes out to the Gentiles. A distinct break with Israel is recorded in 28:28.

The book is often called *transitional* because it covers

the transition from the era of the law to the Church age, from Judaism to Christianity.

(a) Receiving the Holy Spirit

Four communities of believers are found in Acts, and the order of events in connection with the reception of the Holy Spirit is different in each case:

1. In Acts 2:38, *Jews* received the Holy Spirit when they repented and were baptized.
2. In Acts 8:6, 12-17, the *Samaritans* received the Holy Spirit when they believed (v. 6), were baptized (vv. 12, 16), and had the apostles' hands laid on them (v. 17).
3. In Acts 10:44-48, *Gentiles* received the Holy Spirit when they believed (vv. 43-44). After receiving the Spirit, they were baptized (vv. 47-48).
4. In Acts 19:1-6, *some of John's disciples* believed (v. 4), were baptized (v. 5), had Paul's hands laid on them (v. 6), and received the Holy Spirit (v. 6).

The order that applies today is the third one—faith, reception of the Holy Spirit, and baptism.

(b) Acts and Salvation Today

To reiterate, the order that applies in the present day is found in chapter 10. With Israel set aside, the gospel is going out primarily to the Gentiles. The order is (1) faith, (2) reception of the Holy Spirit, and then (3) water baptism. What about Jews who believe today? The order is

71

the same. Israel as a nation has been set aside temporarily, and now *"there is no difference"* (Rom. 3:22b).

(c) THE SOVEREIGNTY OF THE SPIRIT

One of the key lessons in the Book of Acts is the sovereignty of the Holy Spirit. He acts as He chooses, and man cannot fence Him in. He is infinitely varied in the methods He uses, and it is a mistake to try to limit Him to fixed patterns. The symbols of the Spirit—wind, breath, water, fire, cloud—are fluid and unpredictable. So is the Holy Spirit Himself in the Book of Acts.

3. THE EPISTLES

One of the great keys in the study of the epistles is to distinguish between what refers to the believer's *position* and what refers to his *practice.* At least three of the epistles (Romans, Ephesians, Colossians) are structured this way. The early chapters refer to *position,* the latter to *practice.*

A key phrase describing our standing is *"in Christ."* Sometimes the phrase *"in the Lord"* describes our state.

Distinguish between what is fundamental and what is nonessential. In Romans 14:5, Paul says. *"Let each be fully convinced in his own mind,"* meaning that it's a matter of personal choice. There is room for a difference of opinion here. But the apostle is not dealing with the fundamentals of the faith. He is talking about matters of moral indifference, that is, matters of no great importance. Wherever the Bible has spoken by way of commandment, there is no room for individual opinion. But in nonessentials, there is allowance for a difference. Writing to the Corinthians, Paul says, *"I have become all things to all men, that I might by all means save some"* (1 Cor. 9:22b). Does this mean that he was willing to sacrifice biblical principles in order to win the lost? Of course not! It means that he was willing to make any concessions that did not violate God's Word.

In another place, he says, *"To the pure all things are pure"* (Titus 1:15). Taken out of context this could mean that pornography and immorality are pure. But that is false on the face of it. It can only refer to matters that are not sinful or unclean in themselves.

Although the believer is not under law, the New Testament epistles are filled with *commandments* to be obeyed! However, these are not given as law with penalty attached but as instruction for those who have been saved by grace.

Remember, as we have said before: Obedience is the organ of spiritual knowledge (Hos. 6:3; Mt. 13:12). This can't be emphasized too strongly or too often. It's not a person's intelligence quotient that counts; it's his *obedience* quotient!

Some truths must be received by faith because they transcend human understanding. Examples: the Trinity, the union of deity and humanity in the Lord Jesus, election and human responsibility.

Read the text carefully and pay particular attention to the pronouns. In Ephesians 2, the *"you"* in verses 1 and 2 refers to believers of Gentile background, whereas the *"we"* in verse 3 takes in Paul and other Jewish believers. In 1 John 2:28, the thought is,

> *You* [the readers] *abide in Him, so that when He appears, we* [the apostles] *may have confidence and not be ashamed before Him at His coming.*

When the Holy Spirit uses different words, there is generally a different meaning. For example, all believers are children and sons but the words are not synonymous. *Children* means that they are members of God's family. *Sons* means that they are treated as adults with all the privileges and responsibility of mature sons and daughters.

The study of the epistles is enhanced when we also study their historical background in the Book of Acts. For example, in studying Galatians 2:1-10, read Acts 15:1-29. 1 and 2 Timothy find background material in Acts 16:1*ff.*

(a) UNDERSTANDING ROMANS ELEVEN

This is a more crucial chapter than most people realize. That is why we are giving it special attention. A proper interpretation of it is essential to understanding God's program for the future—especially for Israel's future. There are six simple keys:

1. In your thinking add the word "completely" in both verses 1 and 2. The context demands it. God *has* cast away His people but *not completely.* Paul himself is an exception.

2. In your thinking supply the word "finally" in verse

11. Paul does not deny that Israel has fallen; he says in verse 12 that they have. But it is not final. They will be *restored.*

3. Remember that in verses 13-24 the apostle Paul is speaking to Gentiles and not to the Church of God. If you read the Church into this passage, then the Church can be cut off (v. 22). But this is impossible; the members of the Church are sealed for the day of redemption (Eph. 4:30).

4. Remember that the good (cultivated) olive tree (vv. 17-24) represents *the line of privilege* down through the centuries and *not* the nation of Israel. *This is very important!* The natural branches are Israel, the wild olive branches are the Gentiles. Israel was God's chosen people, the original branches in the olive tree. But that nation has been temporarily set aside and the Gentiles are now in the place of privilege. God's present purpose is to call out of the Gentiles a people for His Name (Acts 15:14).

If you take the olive tree to be Israel, then you have Israel growing out of Israel, Israel cast out from Israel, the Gentiles grafted into Israel, the Gentiles possibly cast out of Israel, and Israel grafted back into Israel. Absurd!

5. The fulness of the Gentiles (v. 25) refers to the time when the Gentile bride of Christ is raptured to heaven and God resumes His diplomatic relations with Israel as a nation.

Don't confuse this with *"the times of the Gentiles"* (Lk. 21:24). That's the period during which Israel is dominated by Gentile nations, including today. It closes at the Second Advent of Christ.

6. In your thinking supply the word "believing" in

verse 26. All believing Israel will be saved. We know from other Scriptures that the unbelieving portion of the nation will be destroyed when Christ comes to reign.

4. REVELATION

This is one of the most difficult books of the Bible, also called Apocalypse (*"Unveiling"*). Strangely it is one of the first choices of many who are young Christians. Its imagery is fascinating, intriguing, and beautiful. No wonder people love it.

Here are some simple keys to a not-so-simple book.

1. Realize that the book is primarily a book of judgments, although these are interspersed with many beautiful worship passages, such as chapters 4 and 5.

2. In the first three chapters you have Christ as Judge scrutinizing the churches. This fulfills the dictum that judgment must begin at the house of God.

The letters to the seven churches may be understood as:

- Seven actual churches in John's day. This is certainly true.
- Successive stages or eras in the history of the Church from Pentecost to the Rapture. These do seem to fit the general flow of Christendom's history.
- Features that exist in the worldwide Church at any point in its history on earth. These certainly are helpful insights.

After chapter 3, the church is never once mentioned as being on earth.

3. The main part of Revelation (4:1–19:5) deals with

God's judgments on earth during the Tribulation Period. These judgments are depicted under the symbols of:
- seven seals
- seven trumpets
- seven vials

The seventh seal, trumpet, and bowl all bring you to the end of the Tribulation and the inauguration of Christ's kingdom.

Interspersed among the judgments are numerous parentheses:

a. The 144,000 sealed Jewish saints (7:18).

b. Gentile believers during this period (7:9-17).

c. The mighty angel with the little book (10).

d. The two witnesses (11:3-12).

e. Israel and the dragon (12).

f. The two beasts (13).

g. The 144,000 with Christ on Mount Zion (14:15).

h. The angel with the everlasting gospel (14:6-7).

i. Preliminary announcement of Babylon's fall (14:8).

j. Warning to worshipers of the beast (14:9-12).

k. The harvest and the vintage (14:14-20).

l. The destruction of Babylon (17:11–9:6).

The narrative is not always chronological in Revelation.

4. The final chapters (19:6–22:21) deal with events that follow the Tribulation.

a. The Second Advent of Christ.

b. The Millennium or Thousand-Year Reign of Christ.

c. The Judgment of the Great White Throne.

d. The Eternal State.

5. Generally speaking, it is best to take a passage literally unless it is interpreted as being symbolic in the immediate context or in other parts of the Bible.

Sometimes the meaning is explained right in the context.

    a. The seven stars are angels of the seven churches (1:20).

    b. The seven golden lampstands are the seven churches (1:20).

    c. The great dragon is the devil or Satan (12:9).

In other places, the meaning seems clear from the context:

    a. The rider on the red horse represents warfare (6:3-4).

    b. The third seal is famine (6:5-6).

Sometimes the meaning is explained elsewhere in the Bible. For example, the leopard, bear, and lion (13:2) are identified in Daniel 2 and 7 as the world kingdoms of Greece, Persia, and Babylon. Cruel features of these kingdoms will be found in the beast from the sea.

6. Where no scriptural light can be thrown on a passage, it is best to leave it unexplained until the events take place. There is that feature in Bible prophecy that some things will not be absolutely plain until they occur.

$\mathcal{P}$ROBLEM AREAS

ANTHROPOMORPHISMS

Sometimes characteristics of humans or other creatures are ascribed to God. *"The eyes of the Lord are on the righteous, and His ears are open to their cry"* (Ps. 34:15). *"He shall cover you with His feathers, and under His wings you shall take refuge"* (Ps. 91:4a). God, being Spirit, does not have eyes or ears, and He certainly doesn't have wings and feathers! It helps to have a poetic soul in studying passages like these. The technical name for these is *anthropomorphisms* ("man-forms") and *zoomorphisms* ("living creature-forms").

At times the Bible uses the language of human appearance, that is, how things look to us. When it says that God repents, for instance, it does not mean that He has made a mistake and is sorry for it. His *"repentance"* means that when man moves from obedience to disobedience, for example, God's character requires Him to move from blessing to judgment. In other words, He responds to changes in man in accordance with His own attributes. It looks like repentance to us. Many of these passages are translated *relent* in the NKJV, probably a better word for today.

A theophany is a visible manifestation of God who in

His essence is invisible to mortal eyes. A Christophany is a preincarnate appearance of Christ. When The Angel of the Lord is mentioned in the Old Testament, it is referring to the Lord Jesus (see Gen. 16:11-13; 31:11, 13; Ex. 3:2, 11; Jud. 6:21-22; 13:18, 22; Hos. 12:4-5, cf. Gen. 32:30).

DIVINE PERMISSION

Another helpful insight! God is often said to do what He only permits to be done. This helps us to understand some difficult verses, such as 1 Samuel 16:14: *"...a distressing* [or evil, KJV] *spirit from the Lord troubled him."* No evil can come from the Lord, but He can allow it. Satan robbed Job of almost everything he had, yet Job said, *"The Lord has taken away"* (1:21b). Isaiah quotes the Lord as saying, *"I make peace and create calamity"* [evil, KJV] (45:7b). Because He permits calamity, He is said to create it.

SECONDARY AGENTS

Persons are said to do what an agent does for them. We are told that Joshua read all the curses and blessings to the people of Israel (Josh. 8:35), but we learn from Deuteronomy that it was actually the Levites who did it as his agents (Deut. 27:14).

DIVINE/HUMAN AGENCY

As you study the Scripture, you will notice that there is a curious mingling of the *divine* and the *human*. God does His part, but man must do his as well. Be sure to look at both sides of the arrangement.

You find it in election (Eph. 1:4-5) and human responsibility (Jn. 3:16). God chooses but man must choose as well.

You find it in salvation. It is the Lord who saves (Eph. 2:8-9) but both the Scriptures and our experience tell us that there was a time in our lives when we had to accept Jesus Christ by a definite act of faith.

It is in our security as well. We are kept by the power of God (1 Pe. 1:5); that's the divine side. But *"through faith"* is man's side.

It is only God who can sanctify us (1 Thess. 5:23), but we are commanded to be holy (1 Pet. 1:15-16).

We see it in the matter of service. *"Unless the Lord builds the house, they labor in vain who build it"* (Ps. 127:1). It's easy to see here that both God and man are involved. The lesson in all of this is this, "Don't try to harmonize the tension. Accept both sides of the paradox."

GENERAL TRUTH

Sometimes a verse may state a general truth but there may be exceptions to it. Not all children who obey their parents live to a ripe old age (Eph. 6:13), but the connection is generally true.

THE INTERPRETATION/APPLICATION KEY

Remember that a passage has only one interpretation, but it may have one or more applications. Take Job 23:10b as an example: *"When He has tested me, I shall come forth as gold."* Job is saying that if he is put on trial before God, the verdict will be not guilty. He is innocent of the charges his friends have brought against him. That is the interpretation. But the verse can be applied to refer to the benefits which a believer receives from trials in life. They refine the character, removing the dross until the Refiner sees His image reflected in the gold.

THE GEOGRAPHICAL FACTOR

The Bible is largely written from the geographical perspective of the land of Israel. Thus north means north of Israel. Weather phenomena are those that prevailed in that area. The world often means the Mediterranean world, that is, the Bible Lands. When Paul says that the gospel had come to all the world in his day (Col. 1:6), we don't have to understand that as meaning that the Aztecs and Incas had heard it.

CHRIST IN ALL THE SCRIPTURES

We should look for our Lord in all the Scriptures. Jesus told the Jews that the Scriptures testified of Him (Jn. 5:39). When He walked with the two disciples to Emmaus, he *"expounded to them in all the Scriptures the things concerning Himself"* (Lk. 24:27).

OTHER CONSIDERATIONS

Bishop Middleton said that when a definite article (in the original) precedes the name of the Holy Spirit, it refers invariably to the Person, whereas if there is no article, it refers to His gifts and influences.[11] Thus when Jesus said in John 20:22, literally, *"Receive Holy Spirit"* (there is no article in the original), He was referring to a foretaste or ministry of the Spirit, not to the Person Himself. They did not receive the Holy Spirit until the day of Pentecost.

Notice that while everything in the Bible is truly recounted, not everything quoted is true. Inspiration does not guarantee the truthfulness of what the devil says (Gen. 3:15) or of what man says by his own wisdom (Job 42:7). The Bible says, *"There is no God,"* but it is quoting a fool who is saying it!

Words used in the Bible are often flexible enough to describe things that did not exist at the time they were written. Thus Ezekiel talks about bow and arrow warfare, but the Hebrew words could just as well describe ballistic missiles. Pierson agrees that "an elastic poetic phraseology, obscure and enigmatic, provides for an after accommodation to newly discovered facts."

The law of prior mention means that persons and things may be mentioned before they actually exist. David *mentions* the temple in Psalm 5:7 but he did not live to see the temple erected.

We should resist the temptation to look at the Old Testament through Christian eyes. We will find many things there that are subChristian. For example, the wholesale destruction of the Canaanites.

Also, we should remember that the Old Testament saints did not have the Bible, as we have. Neither were they permanently indwelt by the Holy Spirit. So we should make allowance for behavior that was irregular but not sinful.

And we should be aware of the fact that God gives an

historical record of many things of which He does *not approve.* Many of the patriarchs were polygamists. That fact is recorded faithfully, but God never approved of multiple wives. He created only one wife, Eve, for Adam. Also some even more lurid forms of sin are mentioned, never in a way to stir the passions, but always in a manner calculated to cause revulsion.

A final thing to remember! Obedience is the organ of spiritual knowledge. The more you obey the Word, the more its treasures will open up to you.

$\mathcal{H}$ELPS

USING A CONCORDANCE

A well-known professor of Christian education used to say regarding the key components for good Bible study: "You, your Bible, the Holy Spirit, and a concordance."

Every believer would agree on the first three, but why is the concordance so important?

A concordance, as most Bible readers know, is an alphabetical listing of all the words in a book with a phrase containing the word in question, usually abbreviated to the first letter. There are concordances to the major English versions of the Bible, such as the KJV, the NKJV, the NASB, the NIV, and others.

FINDING A VERSE

The most popular use of the concordance is to find a verse that you've heard or learned but can't locate. Suppose you learned in Sunday school the verse that says *"There is one God and one Mediator between God and man."* Let's look for it in Strong's concordance:

---

mediator
Ga   3:19 by angels in the hand of a *m*.   *3316*
        20 a *m* is not...of one, but God is one.   "
        20 is not a *m* of one, but God is one.
1Ti   2: 5 and one *m* between God and men, *3316*
Heb 8: 6 he is the *m* of a better covenant,   "
        9:15 he is the *m* of the new testament,   "
        12:24 Jesus the *m* of the new covenant,   "

Pick the least common word in the verse—obviously not the pronouns, or the words *day, and,* or *night.* The least used word is clearly *mediator.* When you find *mediator,* you will see that it is found seven times in the New Testament. As you scan the verses, you will see that the one you are looking for is in 1 Timothy 2:5.

In the right hand column, you will see the number 3316. At the back of the concordance is a section titled *Greek Dictionary of the New Testament.* By referring to number 3316, you will learn which Greek word is translated *mediator.*

Young's concordance is a little different. Here you don't have to refer to some number in the back. It tells you right away that *mediator* is the translation of the Greek word *mesites.*

MEDIATOR —
Middle man, mediator, μεσίτης *mesitēs.*
Gal.   3.19 ordained by angels in the hand of a med.
          3.20 Now a mediator is not..of one; but God
1 Ti.   2. 5 and one mediator between God and men
Heb. 8. 6 he is the mediator of a better covenant
          9.15 for this cause he is the mediator of the
          12.24 to Jesus the mediator of the new covenant

And if several Greek words had been translated *medi-*

ator, it would list all usages separately according to the Greek word.

WORD STUDIES

The fact that a concordance lists all the usages of a significant word in biblical order. is very helpful. It shows how important a word may be in the Bible. For example, *worship, worshiped, worshiper(s), and worships* all together occur nearly 200 times. Clearly worship is an important subject to the One who inspired the Holy Scriptures.

Another clue to a word's *biblical* meaning is often what is called the "law of first reference." Many times there is a helpful start for meditation by seeing where a word is first used.

Worship, for example, first occurs in Genesis 22:5: The lad and I will go yonder and *w.*" Look it up: Abraham and Isaac picture the Father's love in His willingness to sacrifice His Son. This is the center of Christian worship: the cross of Christ, especially as commemorated in the Lord's Supper. Abraham and Isaac are a type, or illustration of God the Father and Christ the Son.

ORIGINAL WORDS

Though some seem to think the English Bible (especially the KJV) is practically the original text, better-informed believers realize that God inspired His Word centuries ago in Hebrew (and a little in Aramaic) in the Old Testament and Greek in the New.

Since the Old and New Testaments were written in different languages, obviously the words lying behind a word will be different in the two Testaments. For a person who does not know Greek, *Vine's Complete Expository Dictionary of Old and New Testament Words* is helpful and instructive. Here, for example, is his treatment of the word *mediator.*

MEDIATOR

mesitēs (μεσίτης, 3316), lit., "a go-between" (from *mesos,* "middle," and *eimi,* "to go"), is used in two ways in the NT, (*a*) "one who mediates" between two parties with a view to producing peace, as in 1 Tim. 2:5, though more than mere "mediatorship" is in view, for the salvation of men necessitated that the Mediator should Himself possess the nature and attributes of Him towards whom He acts, and should likewise participate in the nature of those for whom He acts (sin apart); only by being possessed both of deity and humanity could He comprehend the claims of the one and the needs of the other; further, the claims and the needs could be met only by One who, Himself being proved sinless, would offer Himself an expiatory sacrifice on behalf of men; (*b*) "one who acts as a guarantee" so as to secure something which otherwise would not be obtained. Thus in Heb. 8:6; 9:15; 12:24 Christ is the Surety of "the better covenant," "the new covenant," guaranteeing its terms for His people.

In Gal. 3:19 Moses is spoken of as a "mediator," and the statement is made that "a mediator is not a mediator of one," v. 20, that is, of one party. Here the contrast is between the promise given to Abraham and the giving of the Law. The Law was a covenant enacted between God and the Jewish people, requiring fulfillment by both parties. But with the promise to Abraham, all the obligations were assumed by God, which is implied in the statement, "but God is one."¶ In the Sept., Job 9:33, "daysman."¶

THE ENGLISHMAN'S GREEK CONCORDANCE

One of the by-products of the revival of deep biblical study for the masses in the early 1800s is the 1844 work financed and directed by George V. Wigram. Bible lovers can be glad that George V.'s mother didn't say to her husband after child number 19, "I think our family is big enough now, Dear!"

Why? Because the "V." stands for Vicesimus, Latin for "Twentieth." Naming Roman children "Primus, Secundus, Tertius, Quintus, Sextus, etc., was a tradition of ancient Rome—but Vicesimus? That seems a bit much!

Below is a sample, showing his treatment of one of the words translated *workship* but usually translated *glory.* *Doxa* is number 1391 in Strong's concordance:

δόξα, doxa.

ΔΟΞ

Mat. 4: 8. of the world, and the *glory* of them;
6:13. the power, and the *glory*, for ever.
29. even Solomon in all his *glory* was
16:27. in the *glory* of his Father with
19:28. shall sit in the throne of his *glory*,
24:30. with power and great *glory.*
25:31. Son of man shall come in his *glory*,
— sit upon the throne of his *glory:*
Mar. 8:38. cometh in the *glory* of his Father
10:37. on thy left hand, in thy *glory.*
13:26. in the clouds with great power and *glory.*
Lu. 2: 9. the *glory* of the Lord shone round
14. *Glory* to God in the highest, and on
32. the *glory* of thy people Israel.
4: 6. will I give thee, and the *glory* of them:
9:26. when he shall come in his own *glory*,
31. Who appeared in *glory*, and spake of his
32. they saw his *glory*, and the two men
12:27. Solomon in all his *glory* was not
14:10. then shalt thou have *worship* in the
17:18. returned to give *glory* to God, save
19:38. peace in heaven, and *glory* in the highest.
21:27. in a cloud with power and great *glory.*
24:26. to enter into his *glory?*
Joh. 1:14. we beheld his *glory*, the *glory* as of the
2:11. Galilee, and manifested forth his *glory;*
5:41. I receive not *honour* from men.
44. which receive *honour* one of another,
— the *honour* that (cometh) from God only?
7:18. himself seeketh his own *glory:* but he that
seeketh his *glory* that sent him.

Joh. 8:50. I seek not mine own *glory.*
54. It I honour myself, my *honour* is nothing
9:24. said unto him, Give God the *praise:*
11: 4. for the *glory* of God, that the Son
40. thou shouldest see the *glory* of God?
12:41. said Esaias, when he saw his *glory*,
43. they loved the *praise* of men more than the *praise* of God.
17: 5. with the *glory* which I had
22. the *glory* which thou gavest me
24. that they may behold my *glory*,
Acts 7 2. The God of *glory* appeared unto
55. saw the *glory* of God, and Jesus
12:23. because he gave not God the *glory:*
22:11. for the *glory* of that light, being
Ro. 1:23. the *glory* of the uncorruptible God
2: 7. in well doing seek for *glory* and honour
10. *glory*, honour, and peace, to every man
3: 7. through my lie unto his *glory;*
23. come short of the *glory* of God;
4:20. was strong in faith, giving *glory* to God
5: 2. rejoice in hope of the *glory* of God.
6: 4. by the *glory* of the Father,
8:18. the *glory* which shall be revealed
21. into the *glorious* liberty (lit. liberty of the *glory*) of the children of God.
9· 4. the adoption, and the *glory*, and the covenants,
23. make known the riches of his *glory* on
— had afore prepared unto *glory*,
11:36. to whom (be) *glory* for ever.

A copy belonging to the editor of the second edition (1844 also) is inscribed "Eliz^th Wilson" (even names were abbreviated!). This beautifully illustrates what Mr. Wigram was striving for: every believer—men, women, and even children students of the Word—not just clergymen or theology students at Oxford, Cambridge, and Trinity, Dublin.

This work—still in print over 150 years later, puts the

Greek words (in Greek letters as well as transliterated into English letters) in alphabetical order, but the part of the verse reproduced is in English, with the word or words translating it in italics. One looks up the English word in the index in the back to find out where to locate the word. Looking up our word worship, we find that this word translates five different Greek words, listed with the pages on which they occur. In the index they are in the Greek alphabet, but on the pages where they are listed the Greek is also transliterated. For example, latreuõ is on page 449. It occurs 21 times and is translated not only as "worship" but also as "serve" and "do service." This suggests that worship is more than just reciting a liturgy.

We may also notice the letters latr- at the start of the verb. English uses this in words ending in "-latry," such as Mario*latry*, "the adoration of Mary." To find deeper meanings of these several words translated (in the KJV) as *worship,* you will find *Vine's Expository Dictionary* is most helpful and instructive.

It should be noticed that Wigram's text is based on the Greek Textus Receptus and the Authorized King James Version. The variation in text between the traditional Greek text and more recent editions is variously approximated at as low as 2% and as high as 8%.

BIBLE DICTIONARIES

If you want to make a study of a Bible place such as Jerusalem, Syria, Edom, Antioch, or Rome, you can look up all the verses where that place is mentioned and learn quite a lot about it. This is also true of things (trees, animals, plants, tools, etc.), and, of course, people—whether tribes, nationalities, or named individuals.

But perhaps you want more background information to enrich your comprehension of the biblical context. Maybe you want to know what an ancient wine press looked like, or an onager, or Solomon's Temple.

Older Bible dictionaries, like older English dictionaries, had little black and white pen sketches of things that are much easier to picture than to describe *(tunic, mulberry tree, hyena, for examples.)*

Newer Bible dictionaries often have color and/or black and white photographs from Bible lands, maps, and color paintings of objects that no longer exist, such as Herod's Temple.

Unfortunately some of the very artistic Bible dictionaries have some liberal, radical, feminist, or other unbiblical interpretations sprinkled among the purely unbiased material. Being aware of these trends is "a word to the wise."

Here is a the treatment of *Demetrius* as found in *Unger's Bible Dictionary.*

DEME′TRIUS (de-mē′tri-us).

1. A silversmith of Ephesus who made "silver shrines of Artemis" (Acts 19:24), i.e., probably, silver models of the temple or of its chapel, in which, perhaps, a little image of the goddess was placed. These, it seems, were purchased by foreigners who either could not perform their devotions at the temple itself or who, after having done so, carried them away as memorials or for purposes of worship. Demetrius, becoming alarmed at the progress of the gospel under the preaching of Paul, assembled his fellow-craftsmen and incited a tumult by haranguing them on the danger that threatened the worship of Artemis and, consequently, the profits of their craft. The tumult was quieted by the tact and boldness of the town-clerk, and Paul departed for Macedonia, A.D. (perhaps autumn) 55.

2. A Christian mentioned with commendation in 3 John 12, A.D. about 90. Further than this nothing is known of him.

The grand-daddy of all Bible dictionaries is the

International Standard Bible Encyclopaedia. Just to show how helpful it can be, here is its explanation of why the Lord cursed the fig tree (Mt. 21:18-20; Mk. 11:12, 13, 20, 21) even though the time of the fig crop had not yet come.

The miracle of Our Lord (Mt **21** 18–20; Mk **11** 12.13.20.21) which occurred in the Passover season, about April, will be understood (as far **5. The** as the natural phenomena are con- **Cursing of** cerned) by the account given above **the Barren** of the fruiting of the fig-tree, as repeat- **Fig-Tree** edly observed by the present writer in the neighborhood of Jerus. When the young leaves are newly appearing, in April, every fig-tree which is going to bear fruit at all will have some *taksh* ("immature figs") upon it, even though "the time of figs" (Mk **11** 13 AV), i.e. of ordinary edible figs—either early or late crop—"was not yet." This *taksh* is not only eaten today, but it is sure evidence, even when it falls, that the tree bearing it is not barren. This acted parable must be compared with Lk **13** 6.9; *now* the time of judgment was surely coming, the fate of the fruit-less Jewish nation was forcibly foretold.

BIBLE ATLASES

One religion founded in the United States in the nineteenth century has a book which the Mormons put out as of equal authority with the Bible. It is full of bloody battles, tribes, named individuals, and supposed places. *Not one* of these events, peoples, tribes, or places (other than those lifted from the King James Bible) has any historical corroboration in secular history, geography, or even tradition.

Not so with the Word of God! Hundreds of cities, countries, rivers, mountains, secular leaders known from beyond the Bible's sacred page, also appear in God's Word.

The late Dr. H. Chester Woodring used to say that *going* to the Holy Land and seeing these places first hand "takes the Bible down off the sky-hooks and plants it on *terra firma.*" Next to a trip to Israel, a good Bible Atlas best shows the layout of the lands of the Bible. Most Bibles have some maps in the back and some have nice little black and white maps where they specifically illustrate some events (the ministry of our Lord, the journeys of Paul, *e.g.*).

But large size maps of the ancient world showing the wanderings of the children of Israel, the Divided Kingdom, Palestine in the time of our Lord, and the location of the seven churches of Revelation help to bring these subjects to life.

If you teach the Bible, large flip maps on a tripod can add real interest to your verbal descriptions. They can be seen and ordered from your local Christian bookstore.

BIBLE COMMENTARIES

Any famous book can have comments printed about it. Before his conversion John Calvin, *e.g.,* wrote a commentary on a writing of the Roman Seneca (in Latin!).

There are myriads of commentaries on the Bible, good, bad, and indifferent—especially in English.

Two extremes are to be avoided regarding commentaries. One is to go to the commentaries first and make them the standard for what the Bible teaches. This is not unlike the traditions of the Pharisees or medieval Christendom.

Judge the commentaries by the overall teaching of the Bible, not vice versa.

The other extreme is to reject commentaries altogether. This is just as unreasonable as rejecting the preached Word. For example, the very sound and still popular commentaries of Harry A. Ironside are merely edited versions of his verse-by-verse messages at Moody Church on all the NT books and some OT books. Many of the spiritually insightful works of J. N. Darby, *e.g.,* were not *written* as books, but taken from notes by those who attended "Bible readings." (These "readings" were and are verse-by-verse *discussions* of the Bible, often before a congregation by men steeped (hopefully) in Holy Scripture.)

The Interlinear Key

Many careful Bible students are puzzled over the differences between various English translations of the Bible. Since all languages change over time it is not too hard to see why, for example, the NKJV is more modern than the original KJV (1611, but the 1769 edition is generally used). But why are all the translations made between the 1970s and the 1990s different in wording, word order, and in what is included or omitted?

The interlinear is a helpful tool to check out a translation as to how close it is to the original—or, how far removed! It also generally has a standard translation in small print in the margin to compare.

Interlinears are available using the KJV, RSV, NRSV, NIV, NASB, and NKJV.[12] The line of English translation is given word-for-word between the Greek lines, hence the term "Inter-linear"). The most recent Interlinear is the NKJV Greek-English Interlinear New Testament. Here is the portion covering 1 Timothy 5:1-7.

5 Do not rebuke an older man, but exhort him as a father, younger men as brothers,
2 older women as mothers, younger women as sisters, with all purity.
3 Honor widows who are really widows.
4 But if any widow has children or grandchildren, let them first learn to show piety at home and to repay their parents; for this is good and acceptable before God.
5 Now she who is really a widow, and left alone, trusts in God and continues in supplications and prayers night and day.
6 But she who lives in pleasure is dead while she lives.
7 And these things command, that they may be blameless.
8 But if anyone does not provide for his own, and especially for those of his household, he

c(4:12) NU omits εν πνευματι, in spirit.
a(5:4) TR adds καλον και, good and.

How to Treat Other Believers

5 1 Πρεσβυτέρῳ μὴ ἐπιπλήξῃς,   ἀλλὰ παρακάλει ὡς
  5an 6older 7man 2not 1Do 3rebuke 4sharply, but   exhort him as

πατέρα, νεωτέρους ὡς ἀδελφούς, 2 πρεσβυτέρας ὡς μητέρας,
a father, younger men as brothers,   older women   as mothers,

νεωτέρας   ὡς ἀδελφάς, ἐν πάσῃ ἁγνείᾳ.
younger women as sisters,   with all   purity.

How to Honor True Widows

3 Χήρας τίμα τὰς   ὄντως χήρας. 4 Εἰ δέ τις
widows ˉ Honor the ones really widows. if ˉ But a certain
who really are

χήρα τέκνα ἢ ἔκγονα   ἔχει, μανθανέτωσαν πρῶτον τὸν
widow 2children 3or 4grandchildren 1has, let them learn   first   -

ἴδιον   οἶκον   εὐσεβεῖν   καὶ ἀμοιβὰς ἀποδιδόναι
5their 6own 7house   1to 2show 3piety 4to and payments to give back
household   to make repayment

τοῖς προγόνοις, τοῦτο γάρ ἐστιν a ἀπόδεκτον ἐνώπιον τοῦ
to the parents, this ˉ for is   acceptable before   -
their

Θεοῦ. 5 Ἡ   δὲ ὄντως   χήρα καὶ μεμονωμένη
God. 2the 3one 1Now who is really a widow and having been left alone
she

ἤλπικεν   ἐπὶ τὸν Θεὸν καὶ προσμένει ταῖς δεήσεσι
has set her hope on - God and continues - in supplications

καὶ ταῖς προσευχαῖς νυκτὸς καὶ ἡμέρας. 6 Ἡ   δὲ
and - in prayers night and day. 2the 3one 1But
she who is

σπαταλῶσα, ζῶσα τέθνηκε. 7 Καὶ ταῦτα
living for pleasure, living has died. And these things
is dead while she lives.

παράγγελλε, ἵνα ἀνεπίλημπτοι ὦσιν. 8 Εἰ δέ τις
command, so that 4blameless 1they 2may 3be. if ˉ But anyone

τῶν ἰδίων καὶ μάλιστα τῶν οἰκείων   οὐ προνοεῖ,
- 3his 6own 7and 8especially 9the 10householders 2not 1does 3provide 4for,
his

Since the word-for-word translation is sometimes hard

to understand, where necessary, numbers are provided in this edition over words to help you put the super-literal translation into some semblance of normal English word order. Some other interlinears do the same to a lesser extent.

Even numbered words are not always enough. For example, a grammatical construction that exists in Greek but not in English often is made clearer by a second line that is more idiomatic.

By using these numbers and the second English line, by constant usage an interested student of the Word can build up an idea of Greek structure.

A further help in the NKJV Interlinear consists of Greek word studies in the footnotes tied in with the text where these words access

A person doesn't have to know the Greek alphabet to use an interlinear, but it certainly will make it easier to follow. Fortunately, Greek spelling is regular, so as you learn the pronunciations of the letters, you never have to look up in a dictionary how to pronounce a word.

English vocabulary is 15% Greek in origin (e.g., anchor, apostle, baptize, schedule, telephone, throne), and many of our letters are derived from the Greek.

THE ENGLISH DICTIONARY

Many people don't see how helpful a regular English dictionary can be in clarifying our translations of the Bible.

Average as well as scholarly people have used the ordinary dictionary to good advantage. The beloved Old Testament scholar, Dr. Merrill F. Unger, used to read the dictionary as a book, not just to look up words. Some may say, "But he was a scholar." True, but non-scholars can also benefit greatly from the precise meaning of words.

A teenage immigrant boy from Lower Farstad, part of Norway's southernmost inhabited island, not only practiced saying "3,333" every day in front of a mirror to learn how to say the "th" sound, but he also, like the late Dr. Merrill F. Unger, used to read the dictionary as well, looking up words. By doing this, he developed a better vocabulary than most native-born citizens.

Which dictionary should you use? Several are good, but avoid those that cave in to low standards of language. Dictionaries that list "nu-cu-lar" as acceptable pronunciation of "nu-cle-ar," just because President Eisenhower and Billy Graham (among others) mispronounced it that way, should be avoided.

American Heritage, Oxford Dictionary (there are English and American editions) and some editions of Webster's are good.

Noah Webster (1758-1843) was a devout and scholarly American Christian who learned Sanskrit and other ancient tongues as well as the Greek, Hebrew, and Latin he studied at Yale. He did this in order to produce the first English dictionary anywhere that gave the derivations (technically called the etymology) of the words. His entries often use the Bible for illustrations of English meanings and usage.

The 1824 edition of Webster has many biblical illustrations and usages. Theological words like justification and covenant are correctly defined. It is still possible to obtain copies of this "more Christian" edition, since it has been reprinted in recent years.

SPECIAL STUDIES

BIBLE BIOGRAPHIES

"There's nothing stranger than folks," an American farm-woman once said. She was right. Also, we could put the words *more interesting* in place of the word *stranger.*

The Bible is chock-full of biographies of colorful, cruel, devout, haughty, humble, beautiful, and terrible people. The word *biography* is from the Greek words meaning "life-writing."

Another truth that fits in with biographies is the old saying, "Truth is stranger than fiction." The stories of Joseph, Esther, David, and many more are amazing and yet credible.

Novels that include many "biographies" within them such as Dickens's books have the ring of reality to them. Why? Because they are based on keen observation of real people. All of the biographies in the Bible are true, but they are interpretive to teach divine truth. Much is left out, none is complete.

Some Bible "bios" are short and sweet. For example,

Enoch:

Enoch lived sixty-five years, and begot Methuselah. After he begot Methuselah, Enoch walked with God three hundred years, and had sons and daughters. So all the days of Enoch were three hundred and sixty-five years. And Enoch walked with God; and he was not, for God took him (Gen. 5:21-24).

Jabez:

Now Jabez was more honorable than his brothers, and his mother called his name Jabez, saying, "Because I bore him in pain" And Jabez called on the God of Israel saying, "Oh, that You would bless me indeed, and enlarge my territory, that Your hand would be with me, and that You would keep me from evil, that I may not cause pain!" So God granted him what he requested (1 Chron. 4:9-10).

On the other end of the spectrum there are the four Gospels. These, too, are selective, and stress the last week of our Lord's life, His death, resurrection, and His 40-day post-resurrection ministry.

Most life stories in God's Word are somewhere between Enoch and the Lord Jesus in length.

Such people as Noah, Abraham, Sarah, Jacob, Joseph, Ruth, Hezekiah, Esther, Mary, Peter, Paul, all have enough material to construct nice little bios of them from the text.

Here is how to construct a mini-biography from the text. We have chosen Sarah.

STEP 1: LOOK UP THE PERSON'S NAME IN A CONCOR-
DANCE.

We see right away that *Sarah* occurs many times in the
Bible, chiefly Genesis 17 through 49, but also once in
Isaiah and three times in the New Testament. The possessive form *Sarah's* also occurs, twice in Genesis and once
in Romans.

Below these entries the name Sarai and the possessive
Sarai's occur. We may not have known that this is Sarah's
original name, but when we start reading the first references to Sarah in Genesis 17:15 we find this out. Since
Genesis 11:29 through 17:15 use Sarai, this suggests a
possible major break in her life story.

STEP TWO: LOOK UP, READ, AND JOT DOWN NOTES ON THE
SEVERAL EVENTS IN THE PERSON'S LIFE.

First Passage (Gen. 11:29-31): Sarai marries
Abraham, but is not able to have children.

Second Passage (Gen. 12:5): Sarai leaves for Canaan
with Abraham and the extended family.

Third Passage (Gen. 12:10-20): Beautiful Sarai is
taken into Pharaoh's house after Abraham says she is his
sister (a half truth). God punishes Pharaoh and he sends
Abraham and Sarai on their way.

Fourth Passage (Gen. 16:1-9): Sarai persuades her
husband to bear a child for her by her Egyptian maidser-
vant, Hagar. This was an acceptable custom in those days,
notes and Bible dictionaries tell us. Sarai, despised as

barren by Hagar, deals harshly with her and the poor Egyptian servant flees. She is persuaded to come back under Sarai's authority by the Angel of the Lord.

Fifth Passage (Gen. 17:15-19): God changes Sarai's name to Sarah (*"Princess"*) since He has chosen her to be the mother of the covenant nation in her old age.

Sixth Passage (Gen. 18:6-15): Sarah serves three heavenly visitors at their tent. She laughs while eavesdropping on the news that she will have a son in her old age. Through fear Sarah denies she laughed.

Seventh Passage (Gen. 20:1-18): Through Abraham's deception, Sarah is taken for her beauty by Abimelech, king of Gerar. Again an unbelieving household suffers for the sin of God's servant, Abraham. Sarah herself is rebuked by the king (v. 16).

Eighth Passage (Gen. 21:1-8): Sarah bears Isaac (meaning *"he laughs"*).

Ninth Passage (Gen. 21:9-12): Ishmael scoffs at Isaac so Sarah casts Hagar and him out. God tells Abraham to listen to Sarah's voice since Isaac is the heir of promise.

Tenth Passage (Gen. 23:1-19): Sarah dies at the age of 127 in Kirjath Arba (= Hebron). Sarah is buried in the cave of Machpelah, purchased from Ephron. Study Bible notes or Bible dictionary will tell that Abraham's and Sarah's tomb is still there in Israel. Sarah is mourned by her husband (23:2) and her son, who takes his bride into his mother's tent (24:67). (Gen. 25:12 is not pertinent to Sarah's story.) Sarah is joined in her tomb by Abraham, Isaac and Rebekah, Leah (49:31), and eventually Jacob (50:13).

Eleventh Passage (Isa. 51:1-2): Isaiah calls on the righteous to look to their roots in Abraham and Sarah.

New Testament References to Sarah:

Twelfth Passage (Rom. 4:19): The deadness of Sarah's womb was no impediment to Abraham's faith in God's promise.

Thirteenth Passage (Rom. 9:9): Paul quotes Genesis 18:10 to illustrate that Sarah is the mother of the promised line of the Messiah.

Fourteenth Passage (Gal. 4:21-31): (Note: This important text would not be found in the concordance, since Sarah's name isn't used. Either a cross reference, previous knowledge, a commentary, or Bible dictionary would alert you to its existence.)

Paul uses Sarah and Hagar as an allegory of law and grace, bondage and freedom, flesh and spirit. Sarah has the honor of picturing the *good aspects* in each case.

Fifteenth Passage (Heb. 11:11): Sarah herself is seen as exercising faith to conceive in her old age (some versions re-translate to give Abraham all the credit, but we believe the KJV and NKJV are preferable in light of the last passage).

Sixteenth Passage (1 Pet. 3:5-6): Sarah is listed as a holy woman who trusted in God (faith), and was submissive to her husband's leadership. Her beauty included a quiet spirit (v. 4).

Such women today, Peter tells us, can be called "daughters of Sarah."

STEP THREE: OUTLINE THESE EVENTS AND ELABORATE THE STORIES, STICKING CLOSE TO THE SCRIPTURAL TEXT, BUT ALLOWING HISTORICAL OR ARCHAEOLOGICAL INSIGHTS WHERE VALID.

Major breaking points could be Sarah's Story (Gen. 11-49) and Sarah's Spiritual Legacy (Isa. 51:2 and the New Testament).

Her story could be divided at 17:15 where her name is changed from Sarai to Sarah.

A Sunday school lesson, women's Bible class, message or study, or biographical sermon could all be derived from these jottings.

ILING

Being human, most of us forget things if we don't write them down. As we get older it seems our "forgetories" become more active than our memories.

One solution to this is keeping notebooks of our observations, questions, ideas, *etc.* Serious students of the Word may want to consider a filing system for quotable quotes, helpful explanations of Bible texts, magazine articles, and other information that would help in preaching and teaching.

Normally the filing system would be divided into two sections, one according to books of the Bible and the other according to subjects. In the first you would accumulate helpful explanations of Bible verses or passages and illustrations of Bible texts. The other would contain useful information you might some day want to use on the subject listed.

Most prefer to use ordinary manila file folders. Others use large envelopes made of tyvek (it doesn't rip and lasts for years).

Make photocopies of desired quotations from books you read, documenting each quote with: Name of author, title of book, city and name of publishers, date of publication, and page number.

Example:

Ironside, Harry A. *Expository Messages on the Epistle to the Galatians.* New York: Loizeaux Brothers, 1941. p. 34.

Let the material accumulate in a large file folder labeled "clippings," and file it about twice a year.

Here is a sample list of subjects. It is not to be followed slavishly but is only given to illustrate. We have added asterisks (*) to some subjects that may be needed less by some. Everyone will want to choose his or her own subjects:

Abortion	*Calvinism
Angels	Capital Punishment
Apologetics	Children
Archeology	Christ
*Arminianism	Christian Education
Assurance	Christian Home
Atheism	Christian Life
Attributes of God	Christian Service
Baptism	Christmas
Bible	Church
Bible Study	*Church History
Bible Versions	Comfort
Biographies	Confession
Birth Control	Conscientious Objection

*Counseling
*Covenants
Creation vs. Evolution
Cross
Cults
Deacons
*Denominations
Demonism
Devil
Discipleship
Dispensations
Divorce and Remarriage
Ecumenical Movement
Elders
Eternal Punishment
Eternity
Ethics
Faith
False Teaching
Fasting
Finances
Forgiveness
Funerals
Gifts of the Spirit
Giving
God
Gospel
Grace
Guidance
Healing

Heaven and Hell
*History
History of Israel
Holiness
Holy Spirit
Homosexuality
Inspiration
Jewish Evangelism
Judgment Seat of Christ
Law and Grace
Liberalism/Modernism
Life of Christ
Lord's Day
Lordship Salvation
Lord's Supper
Man
*Maps and Charts
Marriage
Martyrs
Miracles
Miscellaneous
Missions
Mother
Movies
Music
*Neo-Orthodoxy
Pentecostals/Charismatics
Philosophy
Poetry
Politics/Voting

Prayer
Preaching
Prophecy
Psychology
Publicity
Questions
Quiet Time
Rapture
*Reformation
Resurrection
Rewards
Roman Catholicism
Satan
Science
Scripture Memory
Second Coming
Self Esteem
Separation from the World
Sex
Signs and Wonders
Sin

Spiritual Life
*Stewardship of Time
*Suffering
*Sunday School
Tabernacle
Teaching
Television/Internet
Temptation
Thanksgiving
Tongues, Speaking in
*Tracts
Trinity
Typology
*Virgin Birth
Weddings
Women's Ministry
Wonders of God
World Conditions
*World Religions
Worship
Youth

BIBLE MARKING

Another popular way to keep all of our scriptural thoughts in order is to record them in the margins of our Bible and on the blank pages that usually precede and follow the text itself.

Some people may feel a bit uneasy about putting their own thoughts next to the Word of God. However, annotated Bibles such as the Scofield and Ryrie have done this for years and have been a blessing to hundreds of thousands, yes, millions of people. The difference is that this is your study Bible and it will probably never be published.

Regarding a marked Bible there are at least two good methods. One way is to get a Bible with wide margins and neatly write or print in small letters your paragraph headings, observations, and questions in the side or bottom margins and to use this Bible when you hear an expository sermon or a good Bible lesson, as well as for your own studies.

Another view is to keep a totally unmarked Bible for your daily devotions so that you will get "fresh manna" every day. The marked-up study Bible can be used for all other purposes.

COLORED MARKINGS

Even though you are not (probably!) planning to publish your notes in four colors—an expensive process—you can still use several colors for your own purposes.

For example, you might choose blue to mark verses on heaven, red for redemption, purple for the coming kingdom, green for eternal life, etc. The possibilities are endless.

KINDS OF NOTES

Paragraph headings of your own in a printed Bible that lacks them can be a great help in finding passages and cross referencing them. Parallel miracles and events in the four Gospels, for instance, are easy to mark.

When you come to a difficult text that you really don't understand, a little question mark in the margin will be there as a reminder. It may take years on some passages to find a satisfactory understanding, but gradually, as you read, study, hear messages, pray, and meditate, the Bible will more and more interpret itself. After all, the best commentary on the Bible is the Bible itself. It all hangs together because it proceeds from one perfect divine Mind.

UNDERLINING

Simply underlining key words or repeated words makes a page easier to scan the next time. Sometimes two columns of the Bible may have related words or ideas, such as the lost sheep, the lost son, and the lost coin (*cf.*

Lk. 15). These thoughts immediately suggest paragraph headings and a possible Bible lesson (or sermon, if you preach) on "Lostness."

COLLECTED QUOTATIONS

Preachers we hear and books and pamphlets we read often have apt pithy sayings that are worth putting down before you forget them. You may put them on 3x5 cards and keep a box for them. Another popular way to collect them is in the inside and back cover end sheets of your Bible (if white or a light color).

Here are a few examples from the inside covers of the authors' Bibles:

"Gratitude is life's sweetest pleasure" —Luther.
"Humility: Realizing who we are and who God is."
"Unhealthy human relationships make for ineffective divine service."
"God's ways are not our ways."
"Revival: When 'First Peters' become 'Second Peters.'"
"Sanctification: Taking justification seriously."
"The basis of sin is self-sovereignty."
"It's true that God is our Father; but it is also true that our Father is God"—William Kelly.

If the origin is known (as Luther and Kelly above) it is good to give credit. Many of the best sayings, of course, are anonymous.

BIBLE EDITORIAL

There is no punctuation in the ancient manuscripts from which our Bibles have been translated. All such marks were added by later copyists and then by translators and editors. Thus there is a question whether 2 Corinthians 5:19a should read: *"God was in Christ reconciling the world to Himself"* or *"God was, in Christ, reconciling the world to Himself."* According to the first reading, there was some mystical or mysterious way in which God was inside Christ when He accomplished reconciliation. The second (and preferred) meaning is that God was reconciling the world unto Himself, but He was doing it in the Person and work of the Lord Jesus.

CAPITALIZATION

There is no differentiation between capital letters and small letters in the oldest Bible manuscripts. Often we have to judge by the context whether it should be *spirit* or *Spirit,* the latter meaning the Holy Spirit.

CHAPTER AND VERSE DIVISIONS

We can be grateful that the chapter and verse numbering of our Bibles was added by early scholars in order to facilitate location of a passage. However, chapter divisions sometimes interrupt or obscure the flow of thought. For example, see Mt. 9:38; 10:1; Mt. 16:28; 17:1; Mt. 19:30; 20:1; Rom. 14:23; 15:1; 1 Cor. 10:33; 11:1; 1 Cor. 12:31; 13:1; 2 Cor. 4:18; 5:1; 2 Cor. 6:18; 7:1.

SINGULAR AND PLURAL

In the King James Version of the Bible, the words *thee, thy, thine* are singular whereas *you, your, yours* are plural. In all versions, these words are not always stated but are implied when a verb is used. For instance, in 1 Corinthians 12:31, Paul says, *"But earnestly desire the best gifts."* Here the *you* is implied. The Greek form of the verb *desire* is plural. So it refers to the entire assembly, not to an individual. It is useless for an individual to desire a gift because he receives one or more when he is saved. The Spirit distributes them sovereignly, that is, as He wishes (1 Cor. 12:11). But if an assembly feels that it needs someone with a teaching gift, it may pray that the Lord will send such a person to help.

SHADES OF MEANING

Many words have different shades of meaning. For example, the word "perfect" is used in many ways. In Matthew 5:48 we are told be to perfect as our heavenly Father is perfect. Here it means that we should distribute our favors impartially, just as God does. Often it means to be spiritually mature. Generally the context determines the meaning. When applied to believers here on earth, it *never* means sinless.

$\mathcal{T}$HREE IMPORTANT KEYS

ISRAEL AND THE CHURCH

In the closing chapter, I would like to dwell on what I consider to be the three most important keys for the proper understanding of the Scriptures. They are: The difference between Israel and the Church; the dispensations; and the literal interpretation of the Bible.

One of the most important keys in the proper understanding of the Bible is the distinction between Israel and the Church. Failure to recognize this difference leads to all kinds of contradictions and confusion.

In 1 Corinthians 10:32, Paul separates all mankind into Jew, Gentile, and the Church of God. Here he clearly separates the Jew (unbelieving) and the Church. James also draws a line between the Church and Israel in Acts 15 (the Church—a people for His name, v. 14; Israel—the rebuilt tabernacle of David, v. 16).

Israel was God's chosen earthly people. The nation began with Abraham (Gen. 12), and was entered by *natural birth*. Because of its unbelief, Israel is now cast off *for a while* by God (Rom. 11:15a).

The Church is God's chosen heavenly people (1 Pet. 2:9). It began on the Day of Pentecost and is entered by the *new birth*. It is not a continuation of Israel but an entirely new society, one that never existed before. When the Lord Jesus was on earth, He spoke of His Church as future (*"I will build My Church,"* Mt. 16:18). By the time Paul wrote his first letter to the Corinthians, the Church had already been formed (1 Cor. 12:13).

The priesthood of Israel was confined exclusively to *one tribe,* Levi (Deut. 18:1, 5), and to one family, Aaron's (Ex. 28:1). In the Church *all believers* are priests—both holy priests and royal priests (1 Pet. 2:19; Heb. 10:19-22).

"Israel" was not a "mystery," that is, a truth unknown to man, unknowable except by divine revelation, but now made known to the sons of men. The Church *is* a mystery, a secret plan not mentioned in the Old Testament but made known by the apostles and prophets of the New Testament era (Eph. 3:5, 9; Col. 1:25-26; Rom. 16:25-26).

Under the law, a strict separation between Jews and Gentiles was required. The Gentiles were without the Messiah, aliens from the commonwealth of Israel, strangers from the covenants of promise, having no hope and without God (Eph. 2:12). In the Church, believing Jew and believing Gentile are made one new man in Christ (Eph. 2:13-17). They are fellowmembers, fellowheirs, and fellowpartakers of God's promise in Christ through the gospel (Eph. 3:6). Such a unity was unthinkable in the Old Testament.

Although believing Jews under the old covenant had a heavenly hope, the blessings promised to them were largely material blessings in earthly places (see, for example, Deut. 7:12-16; 8:79; 28:1-14). Members of the Church are blessed with all spiritual blessings in the heavenlies (Eph. 1:3).

Israel continues on earth to the end of Christ's kingdom, when the new heavens and the new earth are established. The Church continues on earth until the rapture, when Christ comes and takes His members to the Father's house (Jn. 14:13; 1 Thess. 4:13-18).

There are many other contrasts between Israel and the Church, but these should be enough to show that the two must never be confused.

There are one or two verses that have been used to suggest the identity of Israel and the Church, so we add the following comments.

In Galatians 6:16, Paul says,

And as many as walk according to this rule [that is, the rule of the new creation in v. 15]*, peace and mercy be upon them, and upon the Israel of God."*[13]

Here believing Jews are singled out as a contrast to those false teachers who were trying to mix law and grace for justification. The false teachers claimed to be true Israelites, but the apostle says, "Not so. The true Israelites are those Jews who are saved by grace through faith apart from the works of the law."

Stephen spoke of Israel as the Church (KJV) or congregation (NKJV) in the wilderness (Acts 7:38). The word

translated "church" (*ekklésia*) means any called out company, assembly, or gathering of people. In Acts 19:32 it
even describes a heathen mob! The context determines
when it refers to the Church of God.

The Church is never found in the Old Testament,
except in types, pictures, or symbols. It is not found in the
Olivet Discourse, as explained under "The Olivet
Discourse Key" in Part Two. And the Church is never
seen on earth after chapter 3 of the book of Revelation.

The last trumpet in 1 Corinthians 15:52 sounds for the
Church; it is a trumpet announcing the rapture of the
church. The seventh trumpet of Revelation 11:15 signals
the end of the Tribulation and the inauguration of Christ's
kingdom on earth.

The elect in Matthew 24:22 are God's Jewish elect during the Tribulation. They are not the same as the elect
who constitute the Church (1 Pet. 1:2; 2:9).

THE DISPENSATIONS

Also distinguish the dispensations. Although God does
not change, His methods and policies in connection with
mankind often do. The fact that we are not commanded to
offer animal sacrifices shows that there has been a
change of dispensations. While we can get good out of
everything in the Bible, not everything was written to us.
The old song, "Every promise in the Book is mine, every
chapter, every verse, every line," sounds pious and
upbeat. It has one flaw: It isn't true! All the promises are
not intended for us. For example, the land God promised

Abraham from the Mediterranean to the River Euphrates. That is for the people of Israel, not for the Church.

In different ages, God has tested man under different conditions. We speak of these different administrations as dispensations. (The word translated *dispensation* is the origin of our word *economy.*)

It's similar to what happens in an average household. When a couple first marries, a certain schedule is set up. Then a baby comes along and an entirely new program comes into existence. But this changes again when the child is five or six. And there is a radical difference when that child becomes a teenager, as we all know.

Here are the seven dispensations as widely taught:

1. INNOCENCE

Before Adam—the first man—sinned, he walked in fellowship with God without any jarring note. As long as he remained innocent, he would have continued to live in the garden. But the rebellion of Adam and Eve brought this idyllic dispensation to an end.

2. CONSCIENCE

With the entrance of sin, a new situation prevailed. Fellowship was broken and Adam and Eve were expelled from the Garden of Eden. They learned that a sinful person can approach a holy God only on the basis of a substitutionary sacrifice.

3. HUMAN GOVERNMENT

After the great worldwide flood, God ordained human

government when He ordered capital punishment for a murderer. Although the Bible does not specifically say so, this punishment would not be meted out by a family blood feud but as a result of a proper governmental trial where guilt could be proven.

4. PROMISE

Beginning with Abraham, the Lord inaugurated a period during which He made lavish promises to the patriarchs and to Israel.

5. LAW

Then from Exodus 20 to the end of the Old Testament, God's earthly people were tested under law. The Ten Commandments were designed to show man his utter inability to merit or earn God's favor by his own efforts, to convict him of sin, and to drive him to the Lord for salvation.

6. THE CHURCH

Whereas *"the law was given by Moses, grace and truth came by Jesus Christ"* (Jn. 1:17). At the present time the Church is God's new society, not under law with penalty attached, but with Christ as the new rule of life.

Following the rapture of the Church, God will pour out His judgments on a world that crucified His Son. This administration, known as the Tribulation, will last seven years. The last half will be the *Great* Tribulation, the worst period of trouble that the world has ever known or will ever know.

7. THE MILLENNIUM

The millennium, or thousand year reign of Christ, will be a dispensation characterized by peace and prosperity. It is the golden age of all time. Some think of the eternal state as God's final dispensation. Sin, sorrow, sickness, and death will be abolished and believers will be with Christ in heaven for eternity.

Contrary to popular accusations, dispensationalists do not believe that there is a different gospel in different ages. Salvation always has been and always will be by faith in the Lord and on the basis of the work of Christ on Calvary's cross. In the Old Testament God saved men by faith in whatever revelation He gave them. As far as we know, they did not know about the coming Savior's substitutionary death; it was still future. But God knew about it and put all the value of Christ's work to their account when they believed. Today we put our faith in the Savior who died for us nearly two thousand years ago.

The careful use of dispensational truth helps us to explain, for instance, why we do not offer animal sacrifices today and why the Old Testament laws concerning clean and unclean foods do not apply to us. But extreme, or "ultra-" dispensationalism can rob us of portions of the Word that are filled with spiritual teaching.

CONCLUSION

We have seen many keys: some general, some specific, that help unlock the Word of God. Fortunately, not all are needed in every passage!

LOGICAL STEPS TO USING THE KEYS

A common Christian scenario is a group of people having a Bible study. There are usually a number of translations and paraphrases. A text is read, often in a circle, with few of the texts matching what is read aloud. Then people give their thoughts. "To me this says I should be more careful with _____."

This is not a good method to getting at what the Bible actually teaches. The group has gone right from the first step—observing (often not even doing that very closely) to the last step, "what it means to *me*," or application. We should apply Scripture to our daily life, by all means, but only after we've found out what it really *means in context.*

Oh, wonderful, wonderful Word of the Lord!
True wisdom its pages unfold,
And though we may read them a thousand times o'er
They never, no never, grow old!
Each line has a treasure, each promise a pearl,
That all, if they will, may secure;
And we know that when time and the world pass away
God's Word shall forever endure.[14]

ENDNOTES

1 William MacDonald, *Believers Bible Commentary: Old Testament* (Nashville, TN: Thomas Nelson Publishers, 1992), editor's introduction.

2 OT: 1183 pp. plus Supplements; NT: 1205 pp.

3 They represent close to half a century of study by the author.

4 Frederick Brotherton Meyer, *Abraham, Friend of God* (London: Lakeland, 1974), p. 127.

5 A. W. Pink, *Gleanings in Genesis* (Chicago: Moody Press, 1922), p. 343. Ada R. Habershon, *The Study of the Types* (Grand Rapids: Kregel Publications, 1974), pp. 169-174.

6 Those who are interested in a complete treatment of the numerical structure of Scripture should see F. W. Grant's multi-volume commentary, *The Numerical Bible* (Loizeaux).

7 In Romans 5:11 (KJV) it really reads reconciliation (*katallagé*) in the original.

8 Some believe that the Shepherd actually *is* Solomon in a rustic disguise, as it were.

9 See Ezek. 1:10; Rev. 4:7.

10 Scarlet dye was obtained from the cochineal worm, which may be referred to in Psalm 22:6.

11 F. E. Marsh, *Fully Furnished,* p. 67.

12 Interlinears can be based on the traditional Greek text (KJV and NKJV) or the modern so-called critical text (RSV, NRSV, NASB, and NIV).

13 The NIV translation "*even* the Israel of God" is biased toward the view that the Church has taken over Israel's place in God's plans.

14 The first stanza of the poem "The Wonderful Word" written by John Newton.

·